CAST IRON COOKING

pil

Publications
International, Ltd.

Photography on pages 13, 21, 59, 73, 99, 107, 143, 153, 157, 161, 169, 179, 181 and 185 by PIL Photo Studio North.

Pictured on the front cover: Chicken Scarpiello *(page 68)*.

Pictured on the back cover *(top to bottom):* Skillet Roasted Root Vegetables *(page 156),* Chorizo Hash *(page 12),* Ginger Plum Tart *(page 180)* and Grilled Prosciutto, Brie and Fig Sandwiches *(page 106)*.

ISBN: 978-1-4508-8141-8

Library of Congress Control Number: 2014930452

Manufactured in China.

8 7 6 5 4 3 2 1

Publications International, Ltd.

CONTENTS

THE NEW IRON AGE

Cast iron pans have been around for hundreds of years, so why all the fuss about them now? The answer is simple: As more and more people are cooking at home, they are rediscovering this old-fashioned cookware and its many strengths. Cast iron is incredibly versatile, durable and inexpensive—what's not to like?

TRIED AND TRUE

If you need more convincing about cast iron pans, consider a few of their finer qualities:

LONGEVITY

Simply put, this pan will last a lifetime. It's easy to find home cooks using their grandmothers' and great-grandmothers' pans; these are often handed down from generation to generation. A quick search on eBay will show you how the value of these older pans has gone up over time.

DURABILITY

It is virtually impossible to put a dent in a cast iron pan. There are no rivets or welded joints to wear out because the pan is cast from a mold in a single piece of metal. And with a good layer of seasoning, it's also impervious to rust and scratches. You can heat it over the highest flames on your stovetop, stick it under the broiler or put it right into the coals of a campfire; the pan will be none the worse for the wear.

VERSATILITY

The range of dishes you can make in this pan is incredible. Start with breads such as corn bread, cinnamon rolls, biscuits or even pizza. Cook up bacon, eggs and hash for hearty breakfasts. Sear meat and seafood beautifully, or fry chicken to perfection. And don't forget dessert! Skillet pies, crisps and cookies are a delicious way to end any meal.

HEAT RETENTION

Dense cast iron pans do take a long time to heat up—far longer than other metals used in cookware such as aluminum or copper. But they don't cool down much when food is added; they maintain a steady heat so foods cook and brown evenly. (That's the key to non-greasy fried food.) The heat in the pan also stays constant in the oven, where temperatures often fluctuate during baking.

NATURAL NONSTICK COATING

A brand new, pre-seasoned pan might not be perfectly nonstick right out of the box, but after regular use, a layer of seasoning will build up and the surface will be as nonstick and smooth as a Teflon-coated pan—without all the chemicals.

INEXPENSIVE

Unless you want to pay a high price for a vintage pan, you can find a large cast iron skillet for around $30 or even less. Compared to the expensive, high-end cookware on the market today, cast iron is an exceptional bargain!

THE PAN THAT CAN

So what exactly can you do with a cast iron pan? Just about anything!

▌**Frying:** Everyone loves fried chicken, but the bird is just the beginning. There are so many other tempting options to explore, from fritters, dumplings and doughnuts to hush puppies and potatoes. Cast iron makes frying simple and foolproof.

▌**Searing:** Your cast iron pan is the secret to getting a beautifully browned crust on steak, chicken, pork, burgers, scallops and more. Whether you're cooking a big roast for a crowd or individual fillets, the results are consistently delicious.

▌**Sautéing:** Almost everything you need for a weeknight meal can be sautéed in a cast iron pan—chicken for quesadillas, vegetables for a stir-fry, blackened shrimp for a po' boy sandwich, sausages for a quick skillet meal, etc.

▌**Braising:** For tougher cuts of meat, low and slow is the way to go. Hearty braised dishes such as short ribs, pork shoulder and beef stew are ideal cast iron comfort foods.

▌**Baking/Roasting:** The ability of cast iron to go from stovetop to oven means the recipe possibilities are endless. You can sear a steak or fish fillet on the stove, then finish cooking it in the oven. You can cook sweet or savory fillings on the stove, top them with a pie crust and bake them in the oven. Or go straight to the oven for beautiful roasted vegetables, whole chicken, fluffy biscuits or an old-fashioned fruit crisp.

▌**Broiling:** If you want to cook a steak or fish fillet in a flash, brown the top of a frittata or get a good crust on a burger without a grill, your cast iron pan and your broiler make a dynamic duo in the kitchen. Chicken and shellfish also fare well under the broiler, and even vegetables—especially peppers, tomatoes and chilies—can get a great smoky charred flavor in minutes.

Whatever you decide to cook, you'll discover that your cast iron pan is simply unbeatable—and worth its weight in gold!

CAST IRON MAINTENANCE

The best way to keep your cast iron pan in good condition is to use it often. You may have heard that cast iron is difficult to care for, but the basics are actually very simple.

▌ Clean the skillet immediately after using it—it is much easier to remove stuck-on food from a hot pan than a cold one. (Just don't soak the pan or leave it in the sink.)

▌ Wash the pan by hand using hot water and a soft sponge. Opinions vary widely about using soap—many believe that soap will strip a pan's seasoning, but others argue that a small amount of today's mild dish soap is completely harmless. Both sides agree that tough abrasives, such as steel wool, rough scouring pads or kitchen cleansers, should always be avoided.

▌ For any stubborn food residue, scrub the pan with a paste of coarse salt and water or coarse salt and oil. You can also loosen stuck-on food by boiling water in the pan for several minutes.

▌ When the pan is clean, dry it thoroughly, reheat it and coat the inside of the pan with a thin layer of oil using a paper towel or a cloth. Store the pan in a dry place.

SEASONING CAST IRON

How does seasoning work? The surface of a cast iron pan is full of tiny cracks, pores and irregularities that food sticks to when cooking. The key to preventing this sticking is fat: When oil is heated in the pan, it polymerizes, which means it forms a dense, slick layer on the surface that makes it seem nonstick. The more times oil is reheated in a pan, the thicker this layer gets.

The vast majority of new cast iron cookware sold today is pre-seasoned, so this additional seasoning process may not be necessary. However, new pre-seasoned cast iron pans will have some sticky spots at first; you can help build up the seasoning by cooking fatty foods the first few times you use the pan.

1. Start out with a clean, completely dry pan. (At this point you can wash the pan with soap since it will be seasoned afterwards.)

2. Rub all surfaces of the pan (inside and outside) with a thin layer of vegetable oil, canola oil, corn oil or shortening using a paper towel or a cloth.

3. Heat the pan in a 450°F oven for 30 minutes or until the surface has darkened in color.

4. Repeat the oiling and heating process three more times until the pan is very dark black. Let the pan cool before storing it in a dry place.

BREAKFAST & BRUNCH

SPINACH FETA FRITTATA

  6 eggs
  ⅓ cup evaporated milk
  1 package (10 ounces) frozen chopped spinach, thawed and squeezed dry
  ½ cup finely chopped green onions
  1½ teaspoons dried oregano or basil
  ½ teaspoon salt
  ⅛ teaspoon black pepper
  2 cups cooked spaghetti (4 ounces uncooked)
  4 ounces crumbled sun-dried tomato and basil or plain feta cheese
  1 tablespoon olive oil
     Diced red bell pepper (optional)

1. Preheat broiler.

2. Whisk eggs and evaporated milk in medium bowl until well blended. Stir in spinach, green onions, oregano, salt and black pepper. Stir in spaghetti and feta cheese.

3. Heat oil in medium cast iron skillet over medium heat. Add egg mixture; cook 5 minutes or until almost set, stirring occasionally.

4. Broil 3 to 5 minutes or until just beginning to brown and center is set. Cut into four wedges. Garnish with bell pepper.

Makes 4 servings

WHOLE WHEAT PANCAKES

¾ cup milk

2 eggs

¼ cup plain Greek yogurt

2 tablespoons vegetable oil

1 tablespoon honey

1 cup whole wheat flour

2 teaspoons baking powder

⅛ teaspoon salt

1 tablespoon butter

Raspberries, blueberries and/or strawberries (optional)

Maple syrup (optional)

1. Whisk milk, eggs, yogurt, oil and honey in medium bowl until well blended. Add flour, baking powder and salt; whisk just until blended.

2. Heat large cast iron skillet over medium heat. Add ½ tablespoon butter; brush to evenly coat skillet. Pour batter into skillet by ¼ cupfuls. Cook about 2 minutes or until tops of pancakes appear dull and bubbles form around edges. Turn and cook 1 to 2 minutes or until firm and bottoms are browned, adding remaining 1½ teaspoons butter as needed.

3. Serve with berries and maple syrup, if desired. *Makes 4 servings*

TIP: To keep pancakes warm while remaining batches are cooking, preheat oven to 200°F and place a wire cooling rack directly on the oven rack. Transfer pancakes to wire rack as they finish cooking. The pancakes will stay warm without getting soggy.

CHORIZO HASH

2 unpeeled russet potatoes, cut into ½-inch pieces
1 tablespoon salt, divided
8 ounces chorizo sausage
1 yellow onion, chopped
½ red bell pepper, chopped (about ½ cup)
   Fried or poached eggs (optional)
   Avocado slices (optional)
   Chopped fresh cilantro (optional)

1. Fill medium saucepan half full with water. Add potatoes and 2 teaspoons salt; bring to a boil over high heat. Reduce heat to medium-low; cook about 8 minutes. (Potatoes will be firm.) Drain.

2. Meanwhile, remove and discard casing from chorizo. Crumble chorizo into large cast iron skillet; cook and stir over medium-high heat about 5 minutes or until lightly browned. Add onion and bell pepper; cook and stir about 4 minutes or until vegetables are softened.

3. Stir in potatoes and remaining 1 teaspoon salt; cook 10 to 15 minutes or until vegetables are tender and potatoes are lightly browned, stirring occasionally. Serve with eggs, if desired; garnish with cilantro and avocado.

Makes 4 servings

TIP

The chorizo sausage and cilantro give this dish a spicy Mexican flavor, but if you can't find chorizo or you prefer Italian sausage, you can use that instead. (Substitute fresh parsley for the cilantro.) The versatility of hash means you can use any leftover meat to make the dish—steak, ham, turkey, chicken, etc. Simply adjust and add seasonings that work with the meat that you're using.

CHERRY AND CHEESE PANINI

    1 tablespoon olive oil

    1 large red onion, thinly sliced

    ¼ teaspoon dried thyme

    2 teaspoons balsamic vinegar

    ⅛ teaspoon salt

    ⅛ teaspoon black pepper

    ½ cup fresh sweet cherries, pitted and chopped

    4 ounces blue cheese, at room temperature

    3 ounces cream cheese, softened

    8 large thin slices Italian or country-style bread

    1 to 2 tablespoons butter

1. Heat oil in large cast iron skillet. Add onion and thyme; cook and stir over medium heat 3 minutes or until onion is tender. Stir in vinegar, salt and pepper, scraping up any browned bits from bottom of skillet. Transfer to medium bowl; stir in cherries. Wipe out skillet.

2. Mash blue cheese and cream cheese in small bowl until blended. Spread evenly over four bread slices. Top each slice with one fourth of cherry mixture (about ⅓ cup) and remaining bread slices.

3. Melt 1 tablespoon butter in same skillet over medium heat. Add two sandwiches; cook 3 to 4 minutes per side or until golden, pressing down on sandwiches with spatula. Repeat with remaining sandwiches, adding additional butter if necessary. *Makes 4 servings*

TIP: Use a blue cheese with minimal blue veins for best results. Heavily veined cheese may cause a grayish tint when mixed with the cherries.

GERMAN APPLE PANCAKE

   1 tablespoon butter
   1 large *or* 2 small apples, peeled and thinly sliced (about 1½ cups)
   1 tablespoon packed brown sugar
1½ teaspoons ground cinnamon, divided
   2 eggs
   2 egg whites
   1 tablespoon granulated sugar
   1 teaspoon vanilla
   ¼ teaspoon salt
   ½ cup all-purpose flour
   ½ cup milk
    Maple syrup (optional)

1. Preheat oven to 425°F.

2. Melt butter in medium cast iron skillet over medium heat. Add apples, brown sugar and ½ teaspoon cinnamon; cook and stir 5 minutes or until apples just begin to soften. Remove from heat; arrange apple slices in single layer in skillet.

3. Whisk eggs, egg whites, granulated sugar, remaining 1 teaspoon cinnamon, vanilla and salt in medium bowl until well blended. Stir in flour and milk until smooth. Pour batter evenly over apples.

4. Bake 20 to 25 minutes or until puffed and golden brown. Serve with maple syrup, if desired.

Makes 6 servings

NOTE: Pancake will fall slightly after being removed from the oven.

FRENCH TOAST WITH ORANGE BUTTER

⅓ cup whipped butter, softened
2 tablespoons orange marmalade
2 teaspoons honey
4 eggs, beaten
½ cup milk
2 tablespoons sugar
1 teaspoon ground cinnamon
1 teaspoon vanilla
¼ teaspoon ground nutmeg
8 ounces French bread, cut diagonally into 8 slices
2 tablespoons vegetable oil
    Powdered sugar (optional)

1. Combine butter, marmalade and honey in small bowl until well blended. Set aside.

2. Whisk eggs, milk, sugar, cinnamon, vanilla and nutmeg in shallow bowl until well blended. Dip bread slices into egg mixture, turning to coat all sides.

3. Heat 1 tablespoon oil in large cast iron skillet over medium heat. Add bread in single layer; cook 3 minutes per side or until golden. Repeat with remaining bread slices, adding additional oil as needed.

4. Serve with orange butter and sprinkle with powdered sugar, if desired.   *Makes 4 servings*

BREAKFAST BISCUIT BAKE

    8 ounces bacon, cut into ½-inch pieces
    1 small onion, finely chopped
    1 clove garlic, minced
    ¼ teaspoon red pepper flakes
    5 eggs
    ¼ cup milk
    ½ cup (2 ounces) shredded white Cheddar cheese, divided
    ¼ teaspoon salt
    ⅛ teaspoon ground black pepper
    1 package refrigerated jumbo buttermilk biscuits (8 count)

1. Preheat oven to 425°F. Cook bacon in large cast iron skillet until crisp. Remove bacon from skillet; drain on paper towel-lined plate. Pour off and reserve drippings, leaving 1 tablespoon in skillet.

2. Add onion, garlic and red pepper flakes to skillet; cook and stir over medium heat about 8 minutes or until onion is very soft. Set aside to cool slightly.

3. Whisk eggs, milk, ¼ cup Cheddar, salt and black pepper in medium bowl until well blended. Stir in onion mixture.

4. Wipe out any onion mixture remaining in skillet; grease with additional bacon drippings, if necessary. Separate biscuits and arrange in single layer in skillet. (Bottom of skillet should be completely covered.) Pour egg mixture over biscuits; sprinkle with remaining ¼ cup Cheddar and cooked bacon.

5. Bake about 25 minutes or until puffed and golden brown.   *Makes 8 servings*

PUFFY PANCAKE

3 tablespoons melted butter, divided
½ cup all-purpose flour
½ cup milk
2 eggs
¼ teaspoon salt
2 bananas, sliced
1 cup sliced strawberries
Chocolate syrup and/or powdered sugar (optional)

1. Preheat oven to 400°F. Pour 2 tablespoons butter into large cast iron skillet; brush butter over bottom and up side of skillet.

2. Whisk flour, milk, eggs, remaining 1 tablespoon butter and salt in medium bowl at least 1 minute or until well blended. Pour batter into prepared skillet.

3. Bake 20 to 22 minutes or until pancake is golden brown and puffed. Remove from oven; immediately fill with fruit. Drizzle with chocolate syrup, if desired. *Makes 4 servings*

APPLE MONTE CRISTOS

4 ounces Gouda cheese, shredded
1 ounce cream cheese, softened
2 teaspoons honey
½ teaspoon ground cinnamon
4 slices cinnamon raisin bread
1 small apple, cored and thinly sliced
¼ cup milk
1 egg, beaten
1 tablespoon butter
Powdered sugar

1. Combine Gouda cheese, cream cheese, honey and cinnamon in small bowl; stir until well blended. Spread cheese mixture evenly on all bread slices. Layer apple slices over cheese mixture on two bread slices; top with remaining bread slices, cheese side down.

2. Whisk milk and egg in shallow bowl until well blended. Dip sandwiches in egg mixture; turn to coat.

3. Melt butter in large cast iron skillet over medium heat. Add sandwiches; cook 4 to 5 minutes per side or until cheese melts and sandwiches are golden brown. Sprinkle with powdered sugar.

Makes 2 sandwiches

Puffy Pancake

BREAKFAST MIGAS

1 small ripe avocado, peeled and diced
1 tablespoon lime juice
6 eggs
2 tablespoons chunky salsa
1 tablespoon olive oil
1 small onion, chopped
1 jalapeño pepper,* seeded and diced
3 corn tortillas, cut into 1-inch pieces
1 medium tomato, halved, seeded and diced
1 cup (4 ounces) shredded Monterey Jack cheese
  Sour cream (optional)
  Chopped fresh cilantro (optional)

*Jalapeño peppers can sting and irritate the skin, so wear rubber gloves when handling peppers and do not touch your eyes.

1. Combine avocado and lime in medium bowl; toss to coat. Lightly whisk eggs and salsa in medium bowl until blended.

2. Heat oil in large cast iron skillet over medium heat. Add onion and jalapeño; cook and stir 2 minutes or until softened. Add tortillas and tomato; cook about 2 minutes or until tortillas are softened and heated through.

3. Pour egg mixture into skillet; cook until eggs are firmly scrambled, stirring occasionally. Remove skillet from heat; stir in cheese.

4. Top migas with avocado; serve with sour cream and cilantro, if desired. *Makes 6 servings*

NOTE: Migas, a Mexican breakfast dish, is traditionally made in a skillet with leftover stale tortillas that are torn into small pieces by hand.

SAWMILL BISCUITS AND GRAVY

GRAVY

> 3 tablespoons canola or vegetable oil, divided
>
> 8 ounces breakfast sausage
>
> 3 tablespoons biscuit baking mix
>
> 2 cups whole milk
>
> ½ teaspoon salt
>
> ¼ teaspoon black pepper

BISCUITS

> 2¼ cups biscuit baking mix
>
> ⅔ cup whole milk

1. Preheat oven to 450°F. Heat 1 tablespoon oil in large cast iron skillet over medium heat. Add sausage; cook and stir until browned, breaking up large pieces. Remove to medium bowl with slotted spoon.

2. Add remaining 2 tablespoons oil to skillet. Whisk in 3 tablespoons baking mix until smooth. Gradually stir in 2 cups milk; cook and stir 3 to 4 minutes or until mixture comes to a boil. Cook 1 minute or until thickened, stirring constantly. Stir in sausage and any accumulated juices; cook and stir 2 minutes. Stir in salt and pepper.

3. Combine 2¼ cups biscuit mix and ⅔ cup milk in medium bowl; stir until well blended. Spoon 8 mounds onto ungreased nonstick baking sheet. Bake 8 to 10 minutes or until golden brown. Serve warm with gravy.

Makes 8 servings

BRATWURST SKILLET BREAKFAST

1½ pounds red potatoes, cut into ½-inch pieces

3 bratwurst links (about 12 ounces), cut into ¼-inch slices

2 tablespoons butter

1½ teaspoons caraway seeds

4 cups shredded red cabbage

1. Place potatoes in microwavable baking dish; cover and microwave on HIGH 3 minutes. Stir; microwave 2 minutes or just until potatoes are tender.

2. Meanwhile, cook sausage in large cast iron skillet over medium-high heat 8 minutes or until browned and cooked through. Drain on paper towel-lined plate. Pour off drippings.

3. Heat butter in same skillet. Add potatoes and caraway seeds; cook 6 to 8 minutes or until potatoes are golden and tender, stirring occasionally. Return sausage to skillet. Stir in cabbage; cover and cook 3 minutes or until cabbage is slightly wilted. Uncover; cook and stir 3 to 4 minutes or just until cabbage is tender.

Makes 4 servings

SPICY CRABMEAT FRITTATA

1 can (about 6 ounces) lump white crabmeat, drained

6 eggs

½ teaspoon salt

¼ teaspoon black pepper

¼ teaspoon hot pepper sauce

1 tablespoon olive oil

1 green bell pepper, finely chopped

2 cloves garlic, minced

1 plum tomato, seeded and finely chopped

1. Preheat broiler. Pick out and discard any shell or cartilage from crabmeat; break up large pieces of crabmeat. Beat eggs in medium bowl. Add crabmeat, salt, black pepper and hot pepper sauce; mix well.

2. Heat oil in large cast iron skillet over medium-high heat. Add bell pepper and garlic; cook and stir 3 minutes or until tender. Add tomato; cook and stir 1 minute. Reduce heat to medium-low. Stir in egg mixture; cook 7 minutes or until eggs begin to set around edges.

3. Broil 4 inches from heat source 1 to 2 minutes or until golden brown and center is set.

Makes 4 servings

Bratwurst Skillet Breakfast

SWEET POTATO AND TURKEY SAUSAGE HASH

    1 mild or hot turkey Italian sausage link (about 4 ounces)
    1 tablespoon vegetable oil
    1 small red onion, finely chopped
    1 small red bell pepper, finely chopped
    1 small sweet potato, peeled and cut into ½-inch cubes
    ½ teaspoon salt
    ¼ teaspoon black pepper
    ⅛ teaspoon cumin
    ⅛ teaspoon chipotle chili powder

1. Remove and discard casing from sausage. Shape sausage into ½-inch balls. Heat oil in large cast iron skillet over medium heat. Add sausage; cook and stir 3 to 5 minutes or until browned. Remove from skillet.

2. Add onion, bell pepper, sweet potato, salt, black pepper, cumin and chili powder to skillet; cook and stir 5 to 8 minutes or until sweet potato is tender.

3. Stir in sausage; cook without stirring 5 minutes or until hash is lightly browned.   *Makes 2 servings*

CORNMEAL PANCAKES

    2 cups buttermilk
    2 eggs, lightly beaten
    ¼ cup sugar
    2 tablespoons butter, melted
    1½ cups yellow cornmeal
    ¾ cup all-purpose flour
    1½ teaspoons baking powder
    1 teaspoon salt
    Fresh blueberries and maple syrup (optional)

1. Whisk buttermilk, eggs, sugar and butter in large bowl until well blended. Combine cornmeal, flour, baking powder and salt in medium bowl; stir into buttermilk mixture. Let stand 5 minutes.

2. Lightly grease large cast iron skillet; heat over medium heat. Pour batter into skillet by ⅓ cupfuls. Cook 3 minutes or until tops of pancakes are bubbly and appear dry; turn and cook 2 minutes or until bottoms are golden. Serve with blueberries and maple syrup, if desired.   *Makes 4 servings*

Sweet Potato and Turkey Sausage Hash

APPETIZERS & SNACKS

CHICKEN GYOZA

    Dipping Sauce (recipe follows)
  4 ounces ground chicken
  ¼ cup finely chopped napa cabbage
  1 green onion, minced
  1½ teaspoons soy sauce
  ½ teaspoon minced fresh ginger
  ½ teaspoon cornstarch
  22 gyoza or wonton wrappers (about half of 10-ounce package)
  2 tablespoons vegetable oil

1. Prepare Dipping Sauce; set aside. Line baking sheet with parchment paper or brush lightly with vegetable oil.

2. Combine chicken, cabbage, green onion, soy sauce and ginger in medium bowl. Add cornstarch; mix well. For each gyoza, place 1 rounded teaspoonful of chicken filling in center of gyoza wrapper. Dampen edges of wrapper with wet finger. Pull edges of wrapper together; press to seal semicircle. Pleat edges of gyoza by making small folds. Place on prepared baking sheet.

3. Heat vegetable oil in large cast iron skillet over medium heat. Add 8 to 10 gyoza to skillet; do not crowd. Cook 3 minutes per side or until golden brown and filling is cooked through. Keep warm in 200°F oven while cooking remaining gyoza. Serve with Dipping Sauce.

Makes 22 gyoza (4 to 6 appetizer servings)

DIPPING SAUCE: Combine ¼ cup soy sauce, 2 teaspoons mirin (Japanese sweet rice wine) and ¼ to ½ teaspoon chili oil in small bowl; mix well.

MOZZARELLA IN CARROZZA

      2 eggs
    ⅓ cup milk
    ¼ teaspoon salt
    ⅛ teaspoon black pepper
      8 slices country Italian bread
      6 ounces fresh mozzarella, cut into ¼-inch slices
      8 sun-dried tomatoes packed in oil, drained and cut into strips
      8 to 12 fresh basil leaves, torn
    1½ tablespoons olive oil

1. Whisk eggs, milk, salt and pepper in shallow bowl or baking dish until well blended.

2. Place four bread slices on work surface. Top with mozzarella, sun-dried tomatoes, basil and remaining bread slices.

3. Heat oil in large cast iron skillet over medium heat. Dip sandwiches in egg mixture, turning and pressing to coat completely. Add sandwiches to skillet; cook about 5 minutes per side or until golden brown. Cut into strips or squares.   *Makes about 8 appetizer servings*

TIP: To serve these sandwiches for lunch instead of as an appetizer, cut them in half instead of squares.

PEPERONATA

      1 tablespoon extra virgin olive oil
      4 large red, yellow and/or orange bell peppers, cut into thin strips
      2 cloves garlic, coarsely chopped
    12 pimiento-stuffed green olives or pitted black olives, cut into halves
      2 to 3 tablespoons white or red wine vinegar
    ¼ teaspoon salt
    ¼ teaspoon black pepper
      Italian or French bread, sliced

1. Heat oil in large cast iron skillet over medium-high heat. Add bell peppers; cook 8 to 9 minutes or until edges begin to brown, stirring frequently.

2. Reduce heat to medium. Add garlic; cook and stir 1 to 2 minutes. *Do not allow garlic to brown.* Add olives, vinegar, salt and black pepper; cook 1 to 2 minutes or until all liquid has evaporated. Serve with bread.   *Makes 4 servings*

Mozzarella in Carrozza

COCONUT SHRIMP

Spicy Orange-Mustard Sauce (recipe follows)

¾ cup all-purpose flour

¾ cup light-colored beer or water

1 egg

¾ teaspoon baking powder

½ teaspoon salt

¼ teaspoon ground red pepper

1 cup flaked coconut

2 packages (3 ounces each) ramen noodles, any flavor, crushed*

20 jumbo raw shrimp, peeled and deveined

2 cups vegetable oil

*Discard seasoning packets.

1. Prepare Spicy Orange-Mustard Sauce; set aside.

2. Whisk flour, beer, egg, baking powder, salt and ground red pepper in medium bowl. Combine coconut and noodles in another medium bowl. Dip shrimp in beer batter; shake off excess. Coat with coconut mixture.

3. Heat oil to 350°F in large cast iron skillet over medium-high heat. Cook shrimp in batches 3 minutes or just until golden, turning once halfway through cooking. Drain on paper towel-lined plate. Serve with Spicy Orange-Mustard Sauce. *Makes 4 servings*

SPICY ORANGE-MUSTARD SAUCE: Whisk ¼ cup coarse grain or Dijon mustard, 2 tablespoons honey, 2 tablespoons orange juice, 2 teaspoons orange peel, ½ teaspoon ground red pepper and ¼ teaspoon ground ginger in small bowl until blended.

TIP: To keep the coating process neater, use one hand to dip the shrimp in the beer batter and the other hand to coat with the coconut mixture.

CORN FRITTERS WITH TOMATO SAUCE

Tomato Sauce (recipe follows)
½ cup all-purpose flour
1 teaspoon sugar
½ teaspoon baking powder
½ teaspoon salt
⅛ teaspoon dried thyme
   Pinch ground red pepper
1 egg
¼ cup half-and-half or milk
1 cup cooked fresh corn or frozen corn, thawed
   Vegetable oil for frying

1. Prepare Tomato Sauce; set aside.

2. Combine flour, sugar, baking powder, salt, thyme and red pepper in large bowl until well blended. Beat egg and half-and-half in small bowl. Add to flour mixture; stir just until blended. Stir in corn.

3. Pour oil into large cast iron skillet to depth of ¼ inch; heat over medium heat until drop of batter sizzles and turns golden in less than 1 minute. Drop batter by rounded tablespoonfuls into hot oil. Cook 3 minutes or until golden; turn and cook 1 minute or until golden brown. Remove fritters from oil with slotted spoon; drain on paper towel-lined plate. Serve with Tomato Sauce. *Makes 4 servings*

TIP: If desired, serve fritters with a chunky mild salsa instead of tomato sauce.

TOMATO SAUCE

1 tablespoon vegetable oil
1 small red onion, very thinly sliced (1 cup)
1 cup grape tomatoes, halved, or canned diced tomatoes, drained
2 teaspoons balsamic or cider vinegar
1 tablespoon capers
¼ teaspoon sugar (optional)
¼ teaspoon salt
⅛ teaspoon black pepper

1. Heat oil in large skillet over medium-high heat. Add onion; cook and stir 3 to 5 minutes or until tender. Add tomatoes; cook about 3 minutes or until very soft.

2. Remove from heat; stir in vinegar, capers, sugar, if desired, salt and pepper. Serve warm or at room temperature.

CHICKEN WINGS WITH CHIVE-CAPER MAYONNAISE

⅓ cup mayonnaise

1 tablespoon minced fresh chives

2 teaspoons capers

¼ teaspoon black pepper, divided

¼ cup all-purpose flour

½ teaspoon paprika, divided

¼ teaspoon salt

2 eggs

½ cup plain dry bread crumbs

12 chicken drummettes (about 1¼ pounds)

2 tablespoons butter

2 tablespoons vegetable oil

1. For Chive-Caper Mayonnaise, combine mayonnaise, chives, capers and ⅛ teaspoon pepper in small bowl; mix well.

2. For chicken, combine flour, ¼ teaspoon paprika, salt and remaining ⅛ teaspoon pepper in large resealable food storage bag. Beat eggs in large shallow bowl. Combine bread crumbs and remaining ¼ teaspoon paprika in another shallow bowl.

3. Add chicken to flour mixture; shake well to coat. Dip chicken in eggs, then roll in bread crumb mixture to coat.

4. Heat butter and oil in large cast iron skillet over medium-high heat until mixture sizzles. Cook chicken in batches 6 to 7 minutes or until browned on all sides, turning occasionally. Reduce heat to low; cook 5 minutes or until chicken is cooked through, turning occasionally. Serve with Chive-Caper Mayonnaise.

Makes 4 to 6 servings

AREPAS (LATIN AMERICAN CORN CAKES)

1½ cups instant corn flour for arepas*
½ teaspoon salt
1½ to 2 cups hot water (120°F)
⅓ cup shredded Mexican cheese blend
1 tablespoon butter, melted

*This flour is also called masarepa, masa al instante and harina precodica. It is not the same as masa harina or regular cornmeal. Purchase arepa flour at Latin American markets or online.

1. Preheat oven to 350°F. Combine instant corn flour and salt in medium bowl. Stir in 1½ cups hot water. Dough should be smooth and moist but not sticky; add additional water, 1 tablespoon at a time, if necessary. Add cheese and butter; knead until dough is consistency of smooth mashed potatoes.

2. Lightly grease large cast iron skillet; heat over medium heat. Divide dough into six to eight equal pieces; flatten and pat dough into 4-inch discs ½ inch thick. (If dough cracks or is too dry, return to bowl and add additional water, 1 tablespoon at a time.)

3. Immediately place dough pieces in hot skillet. Cook 3 to 5 minutes per side or until browned in spots. Remove to baking sheet.

4. Bake 15 minutes or until arepas sound hollow when tapped. Serve warm. *Makes 6 to 8 arepas*

TIP: Freeze leftover arepas in airtight freezer food storage bags.

AREPA BREAKFAST SANDWICHES: Split arepas by piercing edges with a fork as you would English muffins. Fill with scrambled eggs, cheese and salsa as desired.

MANCHEGO CHEESE CROQUETTES

¼ cup (½ stick) butter
1 tablespoon minced shallot or onion
½ cup all-purpose flour
¾ cup milk
½ cup grated manchego cheese or Parmesan cheese, divided
¼ teaspoon salt
¼ teaspoon smoked paprika or regular paprika
⅛ teaspoon ground nutmeg
1 egg
½ cup bread crumbs
¼ to ½ cup vegetable oil

1. Melt butter in medium saucepan over medium heat. Add shallot; cook and stir 2 minutes. Stir in flour; cook and stir 2 minutes. Gradually whisk in milk; cook until mixture comes to a boil. Remove from heat; stir in ¼ cup cheese, salt, paprika and nutmeg.

2. Transfer mixture to small bowl; cover and refrigerate several hours or up to 24 hours.

3. Shape teaspoonfuls of dough into 1-inch balls with lightly floured hands.

4. Beat egg in shallow bowl. Combine bread crumbs and remaining ¼ cup cheese in another shallow bowl. Coat each ball with egg, then roll in bread crumb mixture to coat.

5. Heat ¼ cup oil in medium cast iron skillet over medium-high heat. Cook croquettes in batches until browned on all sides, adding additional oil as needed. Drain on paper towel-lined plate. Serve warm.

Makes 6 servings

NOTE: Cooked croquettes may be kept warm in a 200°F oven up to 30 minutes before serving.

BEER BATTER TEMPURA

1½ cups all-purpose flour
1½ cups Japanese beer, chilled
1 teaspoon salt
Dipping Sauce (recipe follows)
Vegetable oil for frying
½ pound green beans or asparagus tips
1 large sweet potato, peeled and cut into ¼-inch slices
1 medium eggplant, cut into ¼-inch slices

1. Combine flour, beer and salt in medium bowl just until blended. Batter should be thin and lumpy. *Do not overmix.* Let stand 15 minutes. Meanwhile, prepare Dipping Sauce.

2. Pour oil into large cast iron skillet to depth of 1 inch; heat to 375°F over medium heat. Adjust heat to maintain temperature.

3. Dip 10 to 12 green beans in batter; add to hot oil. Cook until light golden brown. Remove to wire racks or paper towels to drain; keep warm. Repeat with remaining vegetables, working with only one vegetable at a time and being careful not to crowd vegetables. Serve with Dipping Sauce.

Makes 4 servings

DIPPING SAUCE

½ cup soy sauce
2 tablespoons mirin (Japanese sweet rice wine)
1 tablespoon sugar
½ teaspoon white vinegar
2 teaspoons minced fresh ginger
1 clove garlic, minced
2 green onions, thinly sliced

Combine soy sauce, mirin, sugar and vinegar in small saucepan; cook and stir over medium heat 3 minutes or until sugar dissolves. Add ginger and garlic; cook and stir 2 minutes. Stir in green onions; remove from heat.

Beer Batter Tempura

MINI MEATBALLS WITH RED PEPPER DIPPING SAUCE

1 bottled roasted red pepper, drained and coarsely chopped
2 cloves garlic, divided
¼ cup mayonnaise
⅛ teaspoon red pepper flakes (optional)
4 ounces ground beef*
4 ounces ground pork*
1 cup plain dry bread crumbs, divided
1 shallot, minced
¼ teaspoon salt
⅛ teaspoon black pepper
1 egg, beaten
¼ cup vegetable oil

*Some supermarkets sell a meatloaf blend of half beef and half pork; use 8 ounces of the blend. Or, if desired, use all pork in this recipe.

1. For dipping sauce, combine roasted red pepper and 1 clove garlic in blender; blend until smooth. Transfer to small bowl; stir in mayonnaise and red pepper flakes, if desired. Set aside.

2. Mince remaining clove garlic. Combine ground beef, ground pork, ¼ cup bread crumbs, shallot, garlic, salt and black pepper in medium bowl. Add egg; mix well.

3. Spread remaining ¾ cup bread crumbs on large plate. Shape meat mixture into 32 to 36 (1-inch) meatballs. Roll meatballs in bread crumbs to coat.

4. Heat oil in large cast iron skillet over medium-high heat. Cook meatballs in batches 8 minutes or until browned on all sides and cooked through (160°F), turning frequently. Drain on paper towel-lined plate. Serve with dipping sauce.

Makes 8 servings

NOTE: The dipping sauce may be prepared and refrigerated up to 4 hours in advance. Allow the sauce to return to room temperature before serving.

LEMON AND GARLIC SHRIMP

¼ cup olive oil
2 tablespoons butter
1 pound large raw shrimp, peeled and deveined
3 cloves garlic, crushed
2 tablespoons lemon juice
½ teaspoon paprika
¼ teaspoon salt
⅛ teaspoon black pepper
2 tablespoons finely chopped fresh parsley
Italian or French bread, sliced

1. Heat oil and butter in large cast iron skillet over medium-high heat until mixture sizzles. Add shrimp and garlic; cook and stir 4 to 5 minutes until shrimp are pink and opaque.

2. Add lemon juice, paprika, salt and pepper; cook and stir 1 minute. Remove from heat; discard garlic. Spoon shrimp and skillet juices into large serving bowl; sprinkle with parsley. Serve with bread for dipping. *Makes 6 to 8 servings*

CROQUE MONSIEUR BITES

8 thin slices firm sandwich bread
4 slices Swiss cheese, halved (about 4 ounces)
4 slices smoked ham (about 4 ounces)
Dash grated nutmeg
2 tablespoons butter, melted

1. Cut crusts from bread. Place four bread slices on work surface. Layer each with half of slice cheese, one slice ham and remaining half of slice cheese; sprinkle with nutmeg. Top with remaining four bread slices. Brush outsides of sandwiches with melted butter.

2. Cook sandwiches in large cast iron skillet over medium heat 2 to 3 minutes per side or until golden brown and cheese is melted. Cut into quarters. *Makes 16 pieces*

TIP: These sandwiches can be prepared ahead of time. Leave sandwiches whole after cooking and refrigerate until ready to serve. Cut into quarters and place on foil-lined baking sheet. Bake in preheated 350°F oven about 8 minutes or until sandwiches are heated through and cheese is melted.

Lemon & Garlic Shrimp

CRISPY TUNA FRITTERS

1 cup corn bread and muffin mix
¼ cup minced onion
2 tablespoons minced pimiento
¼ teaspoon salt
⅛ teaspoon ground red pepper
⅛ teaspoon black pepper
¾ cup boiling water
1 can (9 ounces) tuna packed in water, drained
Vegetable oil for frying

1. Combine corn bread mix, onion, pimiento, salt, red pepper and black pepper in small bowl; mix well. Slowly stir in water. (Mixture will be thick.) Stir in tuna until blended.

2. Pour oil into large cast iron skillet to depth of ½ inch; heat to 375°F over medium heat.

3. Drop batter by tablespoonfuls into hot oil. Cook about 1 minute per side or until golden brown. Drain on paper towel-lined plate. *Makes 30 fritters (about 6 servings)*

SERVING SUGGESTION: Serve fritters with thousand island dressing or tartar sauce.

TIP Make sure the oil is hot before you drop the batter into the skillet—if the fat is not hot enough, then the food will absorb too much oil and be greasy. To test the oil without a thermometer, drop a few pieces of bread or bread crumbs into the skillet. If they start to sizzle immediately, the oil is ready.

QUICK CHICKEN QUESADILLAS

4 boneless skinless chicken breast halves
3 tablespoons vegetable oil
½ teaspoon salt
1 large yellow onion, thinly sliced
8 medium flour tortillas (6 to 8 inches)
3 cups (12 ounces) shredded Cheddar or Monterey Jack cheese
Salsa, sour cream and/or guacamole (optional)

1. Cut chicken into 1×¼-inch strips.

2. Heat 2 tablespoons oil in large cast iron skillet over high heat. Add chicken; cook and stir 3 to 4 minutes or until lightly browned and cooked through. Season with salt. Remove to plate with slotted spoon.

3. Add onion to skillet; cook and stir about 5 minutes or until translucent. Remove from skillet.

4. Heat remaining 1 tablespoon oil in skillet over medium heat. Place one tortilla in skillet; top with one quarter of chicken, onion and cheese. Place second tortilla over filling; press down lightly. Cook quesadilla about 2 minutes per side or until tortillas are browned and cheese is melted. Repeat with remaining tortillas and filling.

5. Cut into wedges; serve with desired toppings.

Makes 8 appetizer servings

FALAFEL NUGGETS

2 cans (about 15 ounces each) chickpeas
½ cup whole wheat flour
½ cup chopped fresh parsley
1 egg, beaten
⅓ cup plus 2 tablespoons lemon juice, divided
¼ cup minced onion
2 tablespoons minced garlic
2 teaspoons ground cumin
1 teaspoon salt, divided
½ teaspoon ground red pepper or red pepper flakes
½ cup canola oil
2½ cups tomato sauce
⅓ cup tomato paste
2 teaspoons sugar
1 teaspoon onion powder

1. Preheat oven to 400°F. Spray baking sheet with nonstick cooking spray.

2. For falafel, drain chickpeas, reserving ¼ cup liquid. Combine chickpeas, reserved ¼ cup liquid, flour, parsley, ⅓ cup lemon juice, minced onion, garlic, cumin, ½ teaspoon salt and red pepper in food processor or blender; process until well blended. Shape into 36 (1-inch) balls; place 1 to 2 inches apart on prepared baking sheet. Refrigerate 15 minutes.

3. Meanwhile, for sauce, combine tomato sauce, tomato paste, remaining 2 tablespoons lemon juice, sugar, onion powder and remaining ½ teaspoon salt in medium saucepan; simmer over medium-low heat 20 minutes, stirring occasionally. Keep warm.

4. Heat oil to 350°F in large cast iron skillet over medium-high heat. Cook falafel in batches until browned. Place on prepared baking sheet; bake 8 to 10 minutes. Serve with warm sauce.

Makes 12 servings

POULTRY

LEMON GARLIC ROAST CHICKEN

4 sprigs fresh rosemary, divided
6 cloves garlic, divided
1 lemon
2 tablespoons butter, softened
2 teaspoons salt, divided
2 large russet potatoes, peeled and cut into ¾-inch pieces
2 onions, cut into 1-inch pieces
2 tablespoons olive oil
½ teaspoon black pepper
1 whole chicken (3 to 4 pounds)

1. Preheat oven to 400°F. Finely chop 2 sprigs of rosemary (about 2 tablespoons). Mince 3 cloves garlic. Grate peel from lemon; reserve lemon. Combine butter, chopped rosemary, minced garlic, lemon peel and ½ teaspoon salt in small bowl; mix well. Set aside while preparing vegetables.

2. Combine potatoes, onions, oil, 1 teaspoon salt and pepper in medium bowl; toss to coat. Spread mixture in single layer in large cast iron skillet.

3. Smash remaining 3 cloves garlic. Cut lemon into quarters. Season cavity of chicken with remaining ½ teaspoon salt. Place garlic, lemon quarters and remaining 2 sprigs of rosemary in cavity; tie legs with kitchen twine, if desired. Place chicken on top of vegetables in skillet; spread butter mixture over chicken.

4. Roast about 1 hour or until chicken is cooked through (165°F) and potatoes are tender. Let stand 10 minutes before carving. Season with additional salt and pepper to taste.   *Makes 4 servings*

CRISPY BUTTERMILK FRIED CHICKEN

2 cups buttermilk
1 tablespoon hot pepper sauce
3 pounds bone-in chicken pieces
2 cups all-purpose flour
2 teaspoons salt
2 teaspoons poultry seasoning
1 teaspoon garlic salt
1 teaspoon paprika
1 teaspoon ground red pepper
1 teaspoon black pepper
1 cup vegetable oil

1. Combine buttermilk and hot pepper sauce in large resealable food storage bag. Add chicken; turn to coat. Marinate in refrigerator 2 hours or up to 24 hours.

2. Combine flour, salt, poultry seasoning, garlic salt, paprika, red pepper and black pepper in another large food storage bag or shallow bowl; mix well. Working in batches, remove chicken from buttermilk, shaking off excess. Add to flour mixture; shake to coat.

3. Heat oil to 350°F in large cast iron skillet over medium heat. Cook chicken in batches 30 minutes or until cooked through (165°F), turning occasionally to brown all sides. Drain on paper towel-lined plate. Keep warm.

Makes 4 servings

NOTE: Carefully monitor the temperature of the oil during cooking. It should not drop below 325°F or go higher than 350°F. The chicken can also be cooked in a deep fryer following the manufacturer's directions. Never leave hot oil unattended.

FAJITAS

⅓ cup fresh lime juice (from 2 or 3 limes)
¼ cup corn or vegetable oil
2 tablespoons Fajita Seasoning Mix (recipe follows)
1 pound chicken or pork, thinly sliced into bite-size pieces
½ white or red onion, cut lengthwise into ½-inch slices
½ green bell pepper, cut lengthwise into ½-inch slices
½ red bell pepper, cut lengthwise into ½-inch slices
    Flour tortillas, heated
    Grated cheese, fresh cilantro, sliced avocado, diced tomatoes and/or salsa (optional)

1. Combine lime juice, oil and 2 tablespoons Fajita Seasoning Mix in large bowl or resealable food storage bag; mix well. Add chicken; turn to coat. Marinate in refrigerator 1 hour.

2. Remove chicken from marinade; discard marinade. Heat large cast iron skillet over medium-high heat. Add chicken, onion and bell peppers; cook and stir over medium-high heat until chicken is cooked through and vegetables are tender.

3. Spoon mixture into warm tortillas; garnish as desired.

Makes 6 servings

FAJITA SEASONING MIX

½ cup chili powder
3 tablespoons ground red pepper
2½ tablespoons garlic powder
2½ tablespoons celery salt
2 tablespoons lemon pepper
1 tablespoon ground cumin
2 teaspoons salt
2 teaspoons dried oregano
2 teaspoons paprika
1 teaspoon ground nutmeg
1 teaspoon firmly packed brown sugar

Whisk all ingredients in medium bowl until well blended. Store in airtight container.

Makes 1⅓ cups

ROASTED CHICKEN THIGHS WITH MUSTARD-CREAM SAUCE

8 bone-in skin-on chicken thighs

¾ teaspoon black pepper, divided

½ teaspoon salt, divided

2 teaspoons vegetable oil

2 shallots, thinly sliced

½ Granny Smith apple, peeled and cut into ¼-inch pieces

½ cup chicken broth

½ cup whipping cream

1 tablespoon spicy brown mustard

½ teaspoon chopped fresh thyme

1. Preheat oven to 400°F.

2. Sprinkle both sides of chicken with ½ teaspoon pepper and ¼ teaspoon salt. Heat oil in large cast iron skillet over medium-high heat. Add chicken, skin side down; cook 8 to 10 minutes or until skin is golden brown. Remove chicken to plate; drain excess fat from skillet.

3. Return chicken to skillet, skin side up. Transfer to oven; roast about 25 minutes or until cooked through (165°F). Remove chicken to clean plate; tent with foil to keep warm.

4. Drain all but 1 tablespoon fat from skillet; heat over medium heat. Add shallots and apple; cook and stir about 8 minutes or until tender. Stir in broth; cook over medium-high heat about 1 minute or until reduced by half, scraping up browned bits from bottom of skillet. Add cream, mustard, thyme, remaining ¼ teaspoon pepper and ¼ teaspoon salt; cook and stir about 2 minutes or until slightly thickened. Spoon sauce over chicken. Serve immediately.

Makes 4 servings

STUFFED CHICKEN FLORENTINE

4 large (6 to 8 ounce) boneless chicken breast halves, skinless if desired
1 cup shredded Asiago or mozzarella cheese
1 package (10 ounces) frozen chopped spinach, thawed and squeezed dry
⅛ teaspoon ground nutmeg
½ teaspoon salt
¼ teaspoon black pepper
2 tablespoons olive oil
2 cloves garlic, minced
2 cups tomato-basil or marinara pasta sauce
2 tablespoons chopped fresh basil

1. Preheat oven to 375°F. Soak 8 to 12 toothpicks in water 10 minutes.

2. Use sharp knife to cut horizontal slit in side of each chicken breast half to form pocket. Combine cheese, spinach and nutmeg in medium bowl; mix well. Stuff mixture into pockets; close with toothpicks. Sprinkle chicken with salt and pepper.

3. Heat oil in large cast iron skillet over medium heat. Add chicken; cook 3 minutes or until lightly browned. Turn chicken; add garlic to skillet and cook 3 minutes. Pour pasta sauce over and around chicken.

4. Transfer skillet to oven; bake 12 to 14 minutes or until chicken is no longer pink in center.

Makes 4 servings

TIP Soaking the toothpicks in water prevents them from burning in the oven. Be sure to remove them before serving the chicken!

CHICKEN SCARPIELLO

3 tablespoons extra virgin olive oil, divided
1 pound spicy Italian sausage, cut into 1-inch pieces
1 (3-pound) chicken, cut into 10 pieces*
1 teaspoon salt, divided
1 large onion, chopped
2 red or orange bell peppers, cut into ¼-inch strips
3 cloves garlic, minced
½ cup dry white wine such as sauvignon blanc
½ cup chicken broth
½ cup coarsely chopped seeded hot cherry peppers
½ cup liquid from cherry pepper jar
1 teaspoon dried oregano
   Additional salt and black pepper
¼ cup chopped fresh Italian parsley

*Or purchase 2 bone-in chicken leg quarters and 2 chicken breasts; separate drumsticks and thighs and cut breasts in half.

1. Heat 1 tablespoon oil in large cast iron skillet over medium-high heat. Add sausage; cook about 10 minutes or until well browned on all sides, stirring occasionally. Remove sausage to plate.

2. Heat 1 tablespoon oil in same skillet. Sprinkle chicken with ½ teaspoon salt; arrange skin side down in single layer in skillet (cook in batches if necessary). Cook about 6 minutes per side or until browned. Remove chicken to plate. Drain excess fat from skillet.

3. Heat remaining 1 tablespoon oil in skillet. Add onion and remaining ½ teaspoon salt; cook and stir 2 minutes or until onion is softened, scraping up browned bits from bottom of skillet. Add bell peppers and garlic; cook and stir 5 minutes. Stir in wine; cook until liquid is reduced by half. Stir in broth, cherry peppers, cherry pepper liquid, oregano and additional salt and pepper to taste; bring to a simmer.

4. Return sausage and chicken along with any accumulated juices to skillet. Partially cover skillet and simmer 10 minutes. Uncover and simmer 15 minutes or until chicken is cooked through (165°F). Sprinkle with parsley.

Makes 4 to 6 servings

TIP: If too much liquid remains in the skillet when the chicken is cooked through, remove the chicken and sausage and continue simmering the sauce to reduce it slightly.

CHICKEN PICCATA

3 tablespoons all-purpose flour

½ teaspoon salt

¼ teaspoon black pepper

4 boneless skinless chicken breasts (4 ounces each)

2 teaspoons olive oil

2 teaspoons butter

2 cloves garlic, minced

¾ cup reduced-sodium chicken broth

1 tablespoon fresh lemon juice

2 tablespoons chopped fresh Italian parsley

1 tablespoon capers, drained

1. Combine flour, salt and pepper in shallow bowl. Reserve 1 tablespoon flour mixture for sauce; set aside.

2. Pound chicken to ½-inch thickness between sheets of waxed paper with flat side of meat mallet or rolling pin. Coat chicken with remaining flour mixture, shaking off excess.

3. Heat oil and butter in large cast iron skillet over medium heat until mixture sizzles. Add chicken; cook 4 to 5 minutes per side or until no longer pink in center. Remove to plate; keep warm.

4. Add garlic to skillet; cook and stir 1 minute. Add reserved flour mixture; cook and stir 1 minute. Add broth and lemon juice; cook 2 minutes or until thickened, stirring frequently. Stir in parsley and capers. Spoon sauce over chicken.   *Makes 4 servings*

TIP Capers are the deep green flower buds of a Mediterranean bush that have been preserved in a vinegary brine. They range in size from the tiny nonpareil variety from France to pistchio-size buds from Italy and Spain. Rinse them in cold water to remove any excess salt and brine before using.

BBQ CHICKEN SKILLET PIZZA

1 pound frozen bread dough, thawed
1 tablespoon olive oil
2 cups shredded cooked chicken*
¾ cup barbecue sauce, divided
¼ cup (1 ounce) shredded mozzarella cheese
¼ cup thinly sliced red onion
½ cup (2 ounces) shredded smoked Gouda cheese
Chopped fresh cilantro (optional)

*Use a rotisserie chicken for best flavor and convenience.

1. Preheat oven to 425°F. Roll out dough into 13-inch circle on lightly floured surface. Brush oil over bottom and side of large cast iron skillet; place in oven 5 minutes to preheat.

2. Combine chicken and ½ cup barbecue sauce in medium bowl; toss to coat. Remove hot skillet from oven; press dough into bottom and about 1 inch up side of skillet

3. Spread remaining ¼ cup barbecue sauce over dough. Sprinkle with mozzarella; top with chicken mixture. Sprinkle with half of onion and Gouda cheese; top with remaining onion.

4. Bake about 25 minutes or until crust is golden brown. Garnish with cilantro.   *Makes 4 to 6 servings*

TUSCAN-STYLE SAUSAGE SKILLET

1 tablespoon olive oil
½ cup chopped fresh fennel
½ cup chopped sweet or yellow onion
3 cloves garlic, minced
1 can (about 14 ounces) fire-roasted diced tomatoes
1 package (9 ounces) fully cooked chicken or turkey Italian sausage, cut into ½-inch pieces
¾ teaspoon dried rosemary
1 can (about 15 ounces) navy or Great Northern beans, rinsed and drained
4 cups baby spinach or torn spinach

1. Heat oil in large cast iron skillet over medium-high heat. Add fennel, onion and garlic; cook and stir 5 minutes.

2. Stir in tomatoes, sausage and rosemary; cover and cook over low heat 10 minutes or until vegetables are tender. Stir in beans; cook over medium-high heat until heated through. Add spinach; cover and cook 2 minutes or until spinach is wilted.   *Makes 4 servings*

BBQ Chicken Skillet Pizza

CHICKEN BURGERS WITH WHITE CHEDDAR

1¼ pounds ground chicken
1 cup plain dry bread crumbs
½ cup diced red bell pepper
½ cup ground walnuts
¼ cup sliced green onions
¼ cup light-colored beer
2 tablespoons chopped fresh parsley
2 tablespoons lemon juice
2 cloves garlic, minced
¾ teaspoon salt
⅛ teaspoon black pepper
1 tablespoon vegetable oil
4 slices white Cheddar cheese
4 whole wheat buns
  Dijon mustard
  Lettuce leaves

1. Combine chicken, bread crumbs, bell pepper, walnuts, green onions, beer, parsley, lemon juice, garlic, salt and black pepper in large bowl; mix lightly. Shape into four patties.

2. Heat oil in large cast iron skillet over medium-high heat. Cook patties 6 to 7 minutes per side or until cooked through (165°F). Place cheese on patties; cover skillet just until cheese melts.

3. Serve burgers on buns with mustard and lettuce.

Makes 4 servings

MEXICAN CASSEROLE WITH TORTILLA CHIPS

    1 tablespoon vegetable oil
12 ounces ground turkey
    1 can (about 14 ounces) stewed tomatoes
    1 package (8 ounces) frozen bell pepper stir-fry mixture, thawed
    ¾ teaspoon ground cumin
    ½ teaspoon salt
    ½ cup (2 ounces) finely shredded sharp Cheddar cheese
    2 ounces tortilla chips, lightly crushed

1. Heat oil in large cast iron skillet over medium heat. Add turkey; cook until no longer pink, stirring to break up meat. Stir in tomatoes, bell pepper mixture and cumin; bring to a boil. Reduce heat; cover and simmer 20 minutes or until vegetables are tender. Stir in salt.

2. Sprinkle with cheese and chips.

Makes 4 servings

GREEK LEMON CHICKEN

    2 tablespoons extra virgin olive oil, divided
    2 tablespoons lemon juice
    1 teaspoon grated lemon peel
    1 teaspoon dried oregano
    1 clove garlic, minced
    ¼ teaspoon salt
    ⅛ teaspoon black pepper
    4 boneless skinless chicken breasts (about 4 ounces each)
    1 lemon, cut into wedges (optional)
       Baby spinach leaves (optional)

1. Combine 1 tablespoon oil, lemon juice, lemon peel, oregano, garlic, salt and pepper in large resealable food storage bag. Add chicken; turn to coat. Marinate in refrigerator at least 30 minutes or up to 8 hours.

2. Heat remaining 1 tablespoon oil in large cast iron skillet over medium heat. Remove chicken from marinade; discard marinade. Add chicken to skillet; cook 3 minutes. Turn and cook over medium-low heat 7 minutes or until no longer pink in center.

3. Serve with lemon wedges and spinach, if desired.

Makes 4 servings

Mexican Casserole with Tortilla Chips

PAN-FRIED CHICKEN FINGERS

⅓ cup mayonnaise

1 tablespoon honey

1 tablespoon mustard

1 tablespoon packed dark brown sugar

1½ cups biscuit baking mix

1 cup buttermilk*

1 egg, beaten

12 chicken tenders (about 1½ pounds), rinsed and patted dry

Salt and black pepper to taste

¼ to ½ cup canola or vegetable oil

*Or substitute 1 tablespoon vinegar or lemon juice plus enough milk to equal 1 cup. Let stand 5 minutes.

1. Preheat oven to 200°F or "warm" setting. For dipping sauce, combine mayonnaise, honey, mustard and brown sugar in small bowl; mix well.

2. Place baking mix in shallow bowl. Whisk buttermilk and egg in another shallow bowl until well blended. Coat chicken with baking mix, then with buttermilk mixture. Roll in baking mix again to coat. Place on baking sheet; sprinkle with salt and pepper.

3. Heat ¼ cup oil in large cast iron skillet over medium-high heat. Cook chicken in batches over medium heat 5 to 6 minutes per side or until golden, adding additional oil as needed. Remove chicken to clean baking sheet; sprinkle with additional salt and pepper, if desired. Keep warm in oven.

4. Serve chicken with dipping sauce.

Makes 4 main-dish servings or 12 appetizers

CHICKEN FRICASSEE

1 whole chicken (about 3 to 4 pounds), cut up
½ cup all-purpose flour
1 teaspoon salt
¼ teaspoon black pepper
2 to 3 tablespoons vegetable oil
2 to 3 tablespoons butter
1½ cups chicken broth
¾ teaspoon dried thyme
1½ cups baby carrots or 1-inch carrot slices
1 medium onion, cut into wedges
2 stalks celery, cut into 1-inch slices

1. Remove skin from chicken, if desired. Cut large chicken breasts in half crosswise. Combine flour, salt and pepper in large resealable food storage bag. Add chicken pieces, two or three at a time; shake to coat. Reserve remaining flour mixture.

2. Heat 2 tablespoons oil and 2 tablespoons butter in large cast iron skillet over medium heat until mixture sizzles. Add chicken; cook about 8 minutes per side or until lightly browned, adding remaining 1 tablespoon oil and butter if necessary. Remove to plate.

3. Stir 2 tablespoons reserved flour mixture into skillet; cook and stir 1 minute. Gradually whisk in broth until smooth. Stir in thyme. Return chicken to skillet. Add carrots, onion and celery; bring to a boil. Reduce heat to low; cover and simmer 35 minutes or until chicken is tender.

4. Remove chicken and vegetables to large plate. Bring liquid to a boil; boil gently about 5 minutes or until sauce reaches desired thickness. Serve chicken and vegetables with sauce. *Makes 4 to 6 servings*

SPINACH AND TURKEY SKILLET

8 ounces turkey breast tenderloin or turkey strips
⅛ teaspoon salt
1 tablespoon olive oil
¼ cup chopped onion
2 cloves garlic, minced
⅓ cup uncooked rice
¾ teaspoon Italian seasoning
¼ teaspoon black pepper
1 cup reduced-sodium chicken broth, divided
2 cups packed fresh spinach
⅔ cup diced plum tomatoes
¼ cup shredded Parmesan cheese

1. Cut turkey into bite-size pieces; sprinkle with salt.

2. Heat oil in medium cast iron skillet over medium-high heat. Add turkey; cook and stir until lightly browned. Remove to plate. Add onion and garlic to skillet; cook and stir over low heat 3 minutes or until tender. Return turkey to skillet; stir in rice, Italian seasoning and pepper.

3. Reserve 2 tablespoons broth. Stir remaining broth into skillet; bring to a boil over medium-high heat. Reduce heat to low; cover and simmer 15 minutes. Stir in spinach and reserved broth; cover and cook 2 to 3 minutes or until liquid is absorbed and spinach is wilted. Stir in tomatoes; heat through. Sprinkle with Parmesan cheese.

Makes 2 servings

BALSAMIC CHICKEN

1½ teaspoons fresh rosemary leaves, minced *or* ½ teaspoon dried rosemary
2 cloves garlic, minced
¾ teaspoon black pepper
½ teaspoon salt
6 boneless skinless chicken breasts (about 4 ounces each)
2 tablespoons olive oil, divided
¼ cup balsamic vinegar

1. Combine rosemary, garlic, pepper and salt in small bowl; mix well. Place chicken in large bowl; drizzle with 1 tablespoon oil and rub with spice mixture. Cover and refrigerate 1 to 3 hours.

2. Preheat oven to 450°F. Brush large cast iron skillet with remaining 1 tablespoon oil. Place chicken in skillet; bake 10 minutes. Turn chicken, stirring in 3 to 4 tablespoons water if drippings begin to stick to pan.

3. Bake about 10 minutes or until chicken is golden brown and no longer pink in center. If pan is dry, stir in additional 1 to 2 tablespoons water to loosen drippings.

4. Drizzle vinegar over chicken in skillet. Remove chicken to plates. Stir liquid in skillet, scraping up browned bits from bottom of skillet. Drizzle over chicken.

Makes 6 servings

TIP

To remove the leaves from a sprig of rosemary, hold the stem at the top and run your thumb and forefinger down the stem to strip the leaves from the stem. (This method is quicker than removing the leaves one by one.)

MEAT

HAM AND BARBECUED BEAN SKILLET

1 tablespoon vegetable oil

1 cup chopped onion

1 teaspoon minced garlic

1 can (about 15 ounces) kidney beans, rinsed and drained

1 can (about 15 ounces) cannellini or Great Northern beans, rinsed and drained

1 cup chopped green bell pepper

½ cup packed brown sugar

½ cup ketchup

2 tablespoons cider vinegar

2 teaspoons dry mustard

1 ham steak (½ inch thick, about 12 ounces)

1. Heat oil in large cast iron skillet over medium-high heat. Add onion and garlic; cook and stir 3 minutes. Stir in kidney beans, cannellini beans, bell pepper, brown sugar, ketchup, vinegar and mustard; mix well.

2. Trim fat from ham; cut ham into ½-inch pieces. Add ham to skillet. Reduce heat to low; simmer 5 minutes or until sauce thickens and mixture is heated through, stirring occasionally.

Makes 4 servings

OPEN-FACE STEAK AND BLUE CHEESE SANDWICHES

4 boneless beef top loin (strip) or tenderloin steaks, cut ¾ inch thick
  Black pepper
1 teaspoon olive oil
  Salt
4 slices ciabatta bread
8 thin slices blue cheese

1. Season steaks with pepper. Heat oil in large cast iron skillet over medium heat.

2. Add steaks to skillet; do not crowd. Cook 10 to 12 minutes or until medium-rare (145°F), turning once. Remove to cutting board. Tent with foil; let stand 5 to 10 minutes. Slice steaks; season with salt.

3. Toast bread. Place 2 slices blue cheese on each toast slice; top with steak slices. Serve immediately.

Makes 4 servings

PORK MEDALLIONS WITH MARSALA

2 tablespoons all-purpose flour
1 pound pork tenderloin, cut into ½-inch slices
2 tablespoons olive oil
1 clove garlic, minced
½ cup sweet marsala wine
2 tablespoons chopped fresh parsley

1. Place flour in shallow bowl. Coat pork slices with flour, shaking off excess.

2. Heat oil in large cast iron skillet over medium-high heat. Add pork; cook 3 minutes per side or until browned. Remove to plate.

3. Add garlic to skillet; cook and stir 1 minute over medium heat. Add marsala and pork; cook 3 minutes or until pork is barely pink in center. Remove pork to clean plate. Stir in parsley; simmer 2 to 3 minutes or until sauce is slightly thickened. Spoon sauce over pork.

Makes 4 servings

NOTE: Marsala is a rich, smoky-flavored wine imported from the Mediterranean island of Sicily. This sweet varietal is served with dessert or used for cooking. Dry marsala is served as a before-dinner drink.

Open-Face Steak and Blue Cheese Sandwiches

PORK SCHNITZEL WITH MUSHROOM GRAVY

6 thin-cut boneless pork sirloin chops or boneless pork loin chops* (about 1¼ pounds)
  Salt and black pepper
½ cup plus 1 tablespoon all-purpose flour, divided
2 eggs
1 cup plain dry bread crumbs
2 tablespoons chopped fresh parsley *or* 1 tablespoon dried parsley flakes
¼ cup vegetable oil
4 tablespoons butter, divided
¼ cup finely chopped onion
1 package (8 ounces) sliced button mushrooms
1 cup chicken broth
2 to 3 tablespoons half-and-half

*Pork cutlets can be substituted for the boneless pork chops.

1. Pound pork chops to ⅛-inch thickness between sheets of waxed paper with meat mallet. Season with salt and pepper. Place ½ cup flour in shallow bowl. Lightly beat eggs in another shallow bowl. Combine bread crumbs and parsley in third shallow bowl.

2. Coat pork with flour, then with eggs. Roll in bread crumb mixture to coat.

3. Heat oil and 2 tablespoons butter in large cast iron skillet over medium heat until mixture sizzles. Cook pork in batches 3 minutes per side or until browned. *Do not overcook.* Remove to plate; keep warm.

4. Heat remaining 2 tablespoons butter in same skillet over medium heat. Add onion; cook and stir 1 minute. Add mushrooms; cook and stir 6 to 7 minutes or until mushrooms are lightly browned and most liquid has evaporated. Stir in remaining 1 tablespoon flour; cook 1 minute. Stir in broth; bring to a boil, stirring constantly. Boil 1 minute. Remove from heat; stir in half-and-half.

5. Spoon gravy over pork. Serve immediately.   *Makes 6 servings*

PIZZA CASSEROLE

      2 cups uncooked rotini or other spiral pasta
   1½ pounds ground beef
      1 medium onion, chopped
        Salt and black pepper
      1 can (about 15 ounces) pizza sauce
      1 can (8 ounces) tomato sauce
      1 can (6 ounces) tomato paste
      ½ teaspoon sugar
      ½ teaspoon garlic salt
      ½ teaspoon dried oregano
      2 cups (8 ounces) shredded mozzarella cheese
     12 to 15 slices pepperoni

1. Preheat oven to 350°F. Cook pasta according to package directions; drain.

2. Meanwhile, cook beef and onion in large cast iron skillet over medium-high heat 6 to 8 minutes or until browned, stirring to break up meat. Drain fat. Season with salt and pepper.

3. Combine pasta, pizza sauce, tomato sauce, tomato paste, sugar, garlic salt and oregano in large bowl; mix well. Add beef mixture; stir until blended. Spread half of mixture in skillet; top with 1 cup cheese. Top with remaining beef mixture, cheese and pepperoni.

4. Bake 25 to 30 minutes or until heated through and cheese is melted.   *Makes 6 servings*

TIP When cooking pasta for a casserole, reduce the suggested cooking time by a few minutes. The pasta will continue to cook and absorb liquid in the oven.

PORK TENDERLOIN WITH CHERRY SAUCE

1 tablespoon plus 2 teaspoons olive oil, divided
¼ cup finely chopped shallots
1 pork tenderloin (about 12 ounces)
¼ teaspoon salt
⅛ teaspoon black pepper
1 cup reduced-sodium chicken broth
1 cup frozen sweet cherries, thawed
2 tablespoons finely chopped dried sour cherries (optional)
1 tablespoon balsamic vinegar
1 teaspoon butter
1 teaspoon brown sugar

1. Preheat oven to 350°F. Heat 1 tablespoon oil in large cast iron skillet over medium heat. Add shallots; cook 2 to 3 minutes or until lightly browned. Remove to plate; set aside.

2. Season pork with salt and pepper. Heat remaining 2 teaspoons oil in same skillet over medium-high heat. Add pork; cook about 10 minutes or until browned on all sides.

3. Transfer skillet to oven. Roast about 8 minutes or until 145°F. Remove pork to cutting board; tent with foil to keep warm.

4. Return skillet to stovetop. Add broth, sweet cherries, dried cherries, if desired, and vinegar; cook over medium-high heat, scraping up browned bits from bottom of skillet. Mash cherries with fork; cook 5 to 6 minutes or until liquid is reduced to about ½ cup. Reduce heat to medium; stir in butter and brown sugar until well blended.

5. Slice pork. Spoon sauce over pork; sprinkle with reserved shallots. *Makes 2 servings*

EMERALD ISLE LAMB CHOPS

2 tablespoons vegetable or olive oil, divided
2 tablespoons coarse Dijon mustard
1 tablespoon Irish whiskey
1 tablespoon minced fresh rosemary leaves
2 teaspoons minced garlic
1½ pounds loin lamb chops (about 6 chops)
½ teaspoon *each* salt and black pepper
¾ cup dry white wine
2 tablespoons black currant jam
1 to 2 tablespoons butter, cut into pieces

1. Whisk 1 tablespoon oil, mustard, whiskey, rosemary and garlic in small bowl to form paste. Season lamb chops with salt and pepper; spread paste over both sides. Cover and let stand at room temperature 30 minutes or refrigerate 2 to 3 hours.

2. Heat remaining 1 tablespoon oil in large cast iron skillet over medium-high heat. Add lamb in single layer; cook 2 to 3 minutes per side or until desired doneness. Remove to plate; keep warm.

3. Drain excess fat from skillet. Add wine; cook and stir about 5 minutes, scraping up browned bits from bottom of skillet. Stir in jam until well blended. Remove from heat; stir in butter until melted. Spoon sauce over lamb. *Makes 4 to 6 servings*

PEPPER STEAK

1 tablespoon coarsely cracked black pepper
½ teaspoon dried rosemary
2 beef tenderloin or rib-eye steaks (4 to 6 ounces each)
1 tablespoon butter
1 tablespoon vegetable oil
Salt
¼ cup brandy or dry red wine

1. Combine pepper and rosemary in bowl. Coat both sides of steaks with spice mixture.

2. Heat butter and oil in large cast iron skillet over medium heat until mixture sizzles. Add steaks; cook 5 to 7 minutes per side for medium rare to medium or until desired doneness. Remove to plate. Sprinkle with salt; keep warm.

3. Add brandy to skillet; bring to a boil over high heat, scraping up browned bits from bottom of skillet. Boil about 1 minute or until liquid is reduced by half. Spoon sauce over steaks. *Makes 2 servings*

Emerald Isle Lamb Chops

SAUSAGE AND PEPPERS

Light-colored beer or water
1 pound hot or mild Italian sausage links
2 tablespoons olive oil
3 medium onions, cut into ½-inch slices
2 red bell peppers, cut into ½-inch slices
2 green bell peppers, cut into ½-inch slices
1½ teaspoons coarse salt, divided
1 teaspoon dried oregano
Italian rolls (optional)

1. Fill medium saucepan half full with beer or water; bring to a boil over high heat. Add sausage; cook 5 minutes over medium heat. Drain and cut diagonally into 1-inch slices.

2. Heat oil in large cast iron skillet over medium-high heat. Add sausage; cook about 10 minutes or until browned, stirring occasionally. Remove to plate.

3. Add onions, bell peppers, 1 teaspoon salt and oregano to skillet; cook over medium heat about 25 minutes or until vegetables are very soft and browned in spots, stirring occasionally. Add sausage and remaining ½ teaspoon salt; cook 3 minutes or until heated through. Serve with rolls, if desired.

Makes 4 servings

PORK AND SWEET POTATO SKILLET

1½ tablespoons butter, divided
12 ounces pork tenderloin, cut into 1-inch cubes
¼ teaspoon salt
⅛ teaspoon black pepper
2 medium sweet potatoes, peeled and cut into ½-inch pieces (about 2 cups)
1 small onion, sliced
4 ounces smoked sausage, halved lengthwise and cut into ½-inch pieces
1 small apple, cut into ½-inch pieces
½ cup sweet and sour sauce

1. Melt ½ tablespoon butter in large cast iron skillet over medium-high heat. Add pork; cook and stir 2 to 3 minutes or until pork is no longer pink. Season with salt and pepper. Remove to plate.

2. Add remaining 1 tablespoon butter, sweet potatoes and onion to skillet; cover and cook over medium-low heat 8 to 10 minutes or until tender, stirring occasionally. Add pork, sausage, apple and sweet and sour sauce; cook and stir until heated through.

Makes 4 servings

Sausage and Peppers

TEPPANYAKI

⅓ cup tamari or soy sauce

2 tablespoons mirin (Japanese sweet rice wine)

1 tablespoon lemon juice

1 tablespoon orange juice

⅛ to ¼ teaspoon red pepper flakes (optional)

4 small frozen corn on the cob pieces, thawed

2 to 3 tablespoons vegetable oil

2 medium zucchini or yellow squash, cut diagonally into thin slices

4 ounces shiitake mushrooms, stemmed and cut into thick slices

8 ounces beef tenderloin or top loin steak, thinly sliced crosswise

8 ounces pork tenderloin, thinly sliced crosswise

8 ounces medium raw shrimp, peeled and deveined

1. For dipping sauce, combine tamari, mirin, lemon juice, orange juice and red pepper flakes, if desired, in small bowl; set aside.

2. Preheat oven to 200°F or "warm" setting. Microwave corn according to package directions just until heated through. Heat 2 tablespoons oil in large cast iron skillet over medium-high heat. Brown corn about 2 minutes, turning frequently. Remove to large baking pan in oven to keep warm.

3. Add zucchini to skillet; cook and stir 2 to 3 minutes or until browned and tender, adding additional oil if necessary. Remove to pan in oven to keep warm. Add mushooms to skillet; cook 2 to 3 minutes or until tender. Remove to oven.

4. Add beef to skillet; cook 2 minutes or until browned and tender, adding additional oil as needed. Remove to oven. Add pork to skillet; cook about 3 minutes. Remove to oven. Add shrimp to skillet; cook 2 to 3 minutes or until pink and opaque, stirring occasionally.

5. Serve meat and vegetables with dipping sauce.

Makes 4 servings

SERVING SUGGESTION: Teppanyaki is often served with several dipping sauces. A traditional ponzu sauce, as in this recipe, is usually one of them. You can make a quick ginger dipping sauce by adding minced fresh ginger, sake and a bit of wasabi to tamari or soy sauce.

MILANESE PORK CHOPS

 2 tablespoons all-purpose flour
 ½ teaspoon salt
 ½ teaspoon black pepper
 1 egg
 1 teaspoon water
 ¼ cup seasoned dry bread crumbs
 ¼ cup grated Parmesan cheese
 4 boneless pork loin chops, cut ¾ inch thick
 1 tablespoon olive oil
 1 tablespoon butter
   Lemon wedges

1. Preheat oven to 400°F. Combine flour, salt and pepper in shallow bowl. Beat egg and water in another shallow bowl. Combine bread crumbs and Parmesan cheese in third shallow bowl.

2. Coat pork chops with flour mixture, then with egg mixture. Roll in bread crumb mixture to coat, pressing mixture onto pork. Place on waxed paper-lined plate; refrigerate 15 minutes.

3. Heat oil and butter in large cast iron skillet over medium-high heat until mixture sizzles. Add pork; cook 4 minutes or until golden brown. Turn pork and transfer skillet to oven. Bake 6 to 8 minutes or until cooked through (145°F). Serve with lemon wedges.   *Makes 4 servings*

TIP "Milanese" is a preparation where meat is typically pounded thin, coated with egg and then with bread crumbs and Parmesan cheese, and pan-fried in butter and/or oil. It is commonly prepared with pork or veal, but it can be made with chicken as well.

BEEF TENDERLOIN WITH LEMON BUTTER

2 beef tenderloin (filet mignon) steaks (6 ounces each)
¼ teaspoon salt, divided
⅛ teaspoon black pepper
⅛ teaspoon garlic powder
3 tablespoons butter, softened, divided
1 tablespoon finely minced fresh parsley
¾ teaspoon grated lemon peel
¼ teaspoon dried tarragon
1 tablespoon canola oil

1. Sprinkle both sides of steaks with ⅛ teaspoon salt, pepper and garlic powder. Let stand 15 minutes.

2. Meanwhile, combine 2 tablespoons butter, parsley, lemon peel and tarragon in small bowl; mix well.

3. Heat remaining 1 tablespoon butter and oil in medium cast iron skillet over medium-high heat until mixture sizzles. Add steaks; cook 2 minutes per side. Reduce heat to medium; cook 3 minutes per side or until desired doneness. Top steaks with lemon butter. *Makes 2 servings*

TUSCAN LAMB SKILLET

8 lamb rib chops (1½ pounds), cut 1 inch thick
2 teaspoons olive oil
3 teaspoons minced garlic
1 can (19 ounces) cannellini beans, rinsed and drained
1 can (about 14 ounces) diced Italian-style tomatoes
1 tablespoon balsamic vinegar
2 teaspoons minced fresh rosemary leaves

1. Trim fat from lamb chops. Heat oil in large cast iron skillet over medium heat. Add lamb; cook 4 minutes per side for medium (160°F) or until desired doneness. Remove to plate; keep warm.

2. Add garlic to skillet; cook and stir 1 minute. Stir in beans, tomatoes, vinegar and rosemary; bring to a boil. Reduce heat to medium-low; simmer 5 minutes. Serve with lamb. *Makes 4 servings*

Beef Tenderloin with Lemon Butter

GRILLED PROSCIUTTO, BRIE AND FIG SANDWICHES

- ¼ cup fig preserves
- 4 slices (½ to ¾ inch thick) Italian or country bread
  Black pepper
- 4 to 6 ounces Brie cheese, cut into ¼-inch-thick slices
- 2 slices prosciutto (about half of 3-ounce package)
- ¼ cup baby arugula
- 1½ tablespoons butter

1. Spread preserves over two bread slices. Sprinkle pepper generously over preserves. Top with Brie, prosciutto, arugula and remaining bread slices.

2. Heat medium cast iron skillet over medium heat 5 minutes. Add 1 tablespoon butter; swirl to melt and coat bottom of skillet. Add sandwiches to skillet; cook over medium-low heat about 5 minutes or until bottoms of sandwiches are golden brown.

3. Turn sandwiches and add remaining ½ tablespoon butter to skillet. Tilt pan to melt butter and move sandwiches so butter flows underneath. Cover with foil; cook about 5 minutes or until cheese is melted and bread is golden brown.

Makes 2 sandwiches

STEAK DIANE WITH CREMINI MUSHROOMS

- 1½ tablespoons vegetable oil, divided
- 2 beef tenderloin steaks (4 ounces each), cut ¾ inch thick
- ¼ teaspoon black pepper
- ⅓ cup sliced shallots or chopped onion
- 4 ounces cremini mushrooms, sliced *or* 1 (4-ounce) package sliced mixed wild mushrooms
- 1½ tablespoons Worcestershire sauce
- 1 tablespoon Dijon mustard

1. Heat 1 tablespoon oil in medium cast iron skillet over medium-high heat. Add steaks; sprinkle with pepper. Cook 3 minutes per side for medium-rare or until desired doneness. Remove to plate; keep warm.

2. Add remaining ½ tablespoon oil to skillet; heat over medium heat. Add shallots; cook and stir 2 minutes. Add mushrooms; cook and stir 3 minutes. Add Worcestershire sauce and mustard; cook 1 minute, stirring frequently.

3. Return steaks and any accumulated juices to skillet; cook until heated through, turning once. Serve steaks with mushroom mixture.

Makes 2 servings

Grilled Prosciutto, Brie and Fig Sandwiches

MEXICAN TAMALE SKILLET CASSEROLE

1 pound ground chuck
1 cup frozen corn kernels, thawed
1 can (4 ounces) chopped green chiles
1 can (8 ounces) tomato sauce
½ cup water
1 package taco seasoning mix
½ teaspoon ground cumin
1 cup whole milk
½ cup biscuit baking mix
2 eggs
1½ cups (6 ounces) shredded Monterey Jack cheese or Mexican cheese blend
   Sour cream, sliced olives, chopped tomatoes and/or chopped fresh cilantro (optional)

1. Preheat oven to 400°F. Cook beef in large cast iron skillet over medium-high heat about 6 minutes or until browned, stirring to break up meat. Drain fat. Stir in corn, chiles, tomato sauce, water, taco seasoning and cumin; mix well. Remove from heat; smooth top of mixture into even layer.

2. Combine milk, baking mix and eggs in small bowl; stir until well blended. Spread evenly over beef mixture in skillet.

3. Bake about 40 minutes or until crust is golden and knife inserted into center comes out clean. Sprinkle with cheese; let stand 5 minutes before serving. Serve with desired toppings. *Makes 4 servings*

TIP To lighten up this casserole, substitute ground turkey or chicken for the ground chuck. Or swap out half of the beef for black beans, adding them to the skillet with the corn and chiles. (Drain and rinse canned beans before using.)

PORK CHOPS AND STUFFING SKILLET

    4 thin bone-in pork chops (4 ounces each)
    ¼ teaspoon dried thyme
    ¼ teaspoon paprika
    ⅛ teaspoon salt
    4 ounces bulk pork sausage
    1 tablespoon vegetable oil
    2 cups corn bread stuffing mix
    1 cup diced green bell pepper
    ¼ teaspoon poultry seasoning (optional)
    1¼ cups water

1. Preheat oven to 350°F. Sprinkle one side of pork chops with thyme, paprika and salt.

2. Heat oil in large cast iron skillet over medium-high heat. Add pork, seasoned side down; cook 2 minutes. Remove to plate; keep warm. Add sausage to skillet; cook until no longer pink, stirring to break up meat.

3. Remove from heat; stir in stuffing mix, bell pepper, poultry seasoning, if desired, and water just until blended. Arrange pork, seasoned side up, over stuffing mixture.

4. Cover and bake 15 minutes or until pork is no longer pink in center. Let stand 5 minutes before serving.

Makes 4 servings

SEAFOOD

PAN-ROASTED PIKE WITH BUTTERY BREAD CRUMBS

6 tablespoons butter, divided
2 garlic cloves, minced
⅓ cup plain dry bread crumbs
½ teaspoon salt, divided
4 tablespoons chopped fresh parsley
4 pike or other medium-firm white fish fillets (about 6 ounces each)
⅛ teaspoon black pepper
2 tablespoons lemon juice

1. Preheat oven to 400°F.

2. Heat 2 tablespoons butter in small skillet over medium-high heat. Add garlic; cook and stir 1 minute or just until lightly browned. Stir in bread crumbs and ⅛ teaspoon salt; cook and stir 1 minute. Remove to small bowl; stir in parsley.

3. Heat 1 tablespoon butter in large cast iron skillet over medium-high heat. Sprinkle pike fillets with ¼ teaspoon salt and pepper. Add to skillet, skin side up; cook 1 minute. Remove from heat; turn fish and top with bread crumb mixture. Transfer skillet to oven; roast 8 to 10 minutes or until fish begins to flake when tested with fork.

4. Wipe out small skillet with paper towel; heat over medium heat. Add remaining 3 tablespoons butter; cook 3 to 4 minutes or until melted and lightly browned, stirring occasionally. Stir in lemon juice and remaining ⅛ teaspoon salt. Spoon mixture over fish just before serving.   *Makes 4 servings*

PAN-FRIED OYSTERS

¼ cup all-purpose flour
½ teaspoon salt
¼ teaspoon black pepper
2 eggs
½ cup plain dry bread crumbs
5 tablespoons chopped fresh parsley, divided
2 containers (8 ounces each) shucked fresh oysters, rinsed, drained and patted dry
    or 1 pound fresh oysters, shucked and patted dry
Canola oil for frying
5 slices thick-cut bacon, crisp-cooked and chopped
Lemon wedges

1. Combine flour, salt and pepper in shallow bowl. Beat eggs in another shallow bowl. Combine bread crumbs and 4 tablespoons parsley in third shallow bowl.

2. Coat oysters with flour mixture, then with eggs. Roll in bread crumb mixture to coat.

3. Pour oil into large cast iron skillet to depth of ½ inch; heat over medium-high heat until very hot but not smoking (about 370°F). Add one third of oysters; cook about 2 minutes per side or until golden brown. Drain on paper towel-lined plate. Repeat with remaining oysters.

4. Toss oysters with bacon and remaining 1 tablespoon parsley in large bowl. Serve immediately with lemon wedges.

Makes 4 appetizer servings

FISH TACOS WITH CILANTRO CREAM SAUCE

½ **cup sour cream**
¼ **cup chopped fresh cilantro**
1¼ **teaspoons ground cumin, divided**
1 **pound skinless tilapia, mahimahi or other firm white fish fillets**
1 **teaspoon chipotle hot pepper sauce, divided**
1 **teaspoon garlic salt**
2 **teaspoons canola or vegetable oil**
1 **red bell pepper, cut into strips**
1 **green bell pepper, cut into strips**
8 **corn tortillas, warmed**
2 **limes, cut into wedges**

1. For sauce, combine sour cream, cilantro and ¼ teaspoon cumin in small bowl; mix well. Refrigerate until ready to serve.

2. Cut tilapia fillets into 1-inch chunks; toss with ½ teaspoon hot pepper sauce, remaining 1 teaspoon cumin and garlic salt in medium bowl. Heat oil in large cast iron skillet over medium heat. Add fish; cook 3 to 4 minutes or until fish is opaque in center, turning once. Remove to plate.

3. Add bell peppers to skillet; cook and stir 6 to 8 minutes or until tender. Return fish to skillet with remaining ½ teaspoon hot pepper sauce; cook and stir just until heated through.

4. Spoon mixture into warm tortillas. Serve with sauce and lime wedges. *Makes 4 servings*

TIP

To warm tortillas in the microwave, wrap them loosely in a damp paper towel. Microwave for 30 seconds or until heated through.

BLACKENED SHRIMP WITH TOMATOES AND RED ONION

1½ teaspoons paprika
1 teaspoon Italian seasoning
½ teaspoon garlic powder
¼ teaspoon black pepper
8 ounces small raw shrimp (about 24), peeled with tails left on
1 tablespoon canola oil
½ cup sliced red onion, separated into rings
1½ cups halved grape tomatoes
Lime wedges (optional)

1. Combine paprika, Italian seasoning, garlic powder and pepper in large resealable food storage bag. Add shrimp; shake to coat.

2. Heat oil in large cast iron skillet over medium-high heat. Add shrimp; cook 4 minutes or until shrimp are pink and opaque, turning occasionally. Add onion and tomatoes; cook and stir 1 minute or until tomatoes are heated through and onion is slightly wilted. Serve with lime wedges, if desired.

Makes 4 servings

TUNA MONTE CRISTO SANDWICHES

4 slices (½ ounce each) Cheddar cheese
4 oval slices sourdough or challah (egg) bread
½ pound deli tuna salad
¼ cup milk
1 egg, beaten
2 tablespoons butter

1. Place one cheese slice on each of two bread slices. Top with tuna, remaining cheese and bread slices.

2. Whisk milk and egg in shallow bowl until well blended. Dip sandwiches in egg mixture, turning to coat.

3. Melt butter in large cast iron skillet over medium heat. Add sandwiches; cook 4 to 5 minutes per side or until cheese melts and sandwiches are golden brown.

Makes 2 servings

Blackened Shrimp with Tomatoes and Red Onion

CAJUN BASS

2 tablespoons all-purpose flour

1 to 1½ teaspoons Cajun or Caribbean jerk seasoning

1 egg white

2 teaspoons water

⅓ cup seasoned dry bread crumbs

2 tablespoons cornmeal

4 skinless striped bass, halibut or cod fillets (4 to 6 ounces each), thawed if frozen

1 teaspoon butter

1 teaspoon olive oil

   Chopped fresh parsley (optional)

4 lemon wedges

1. Combine flour and seasoning in shallow bowl. Beat egg white and water in another shallow bowl. Combine bread crumbs and cornmeal in third shallow bowl.

2. Coat bass fillets with flour mixture, then with egg white mixture. Roll in bread crumb mixture to coat.

3. Heat butter and oil in large cast iron skillet over medium heat until mixure sizzles. Add fish; cook 4 to 5 minutes per side or until golden brown and fish is opaque in center and begins to flake when tested with fork.

4. Sprinkle with parsley, if desired. Serve with lemon wedges.

Makes 4 servings

SPANISH PAELLA

6 cups chicken broth

3 tablespoons olive oil

½ pound boneless skinless chicken thighs, cut into bite-size pieces

2 to 3 links chorizo sausage (about 5 ounces), sliced

1 medium onion, chopped

1 red bell pepper, chopped

4 cloves garlic, minced

1 teaspoon saffron threads, minced

1½ cups uncooked white rice

1 can (10 ounces) diced tomatoes with chiles

3 tablespoons tomato paste

½ teaspoon salt

¼ teaspoon black pepper

1 pound large raw shrimp, peeled and deveined (with tails on)

½ pound mussels

½ cup frozen peas, thawed

1. Bring broth to a boil in medium saucepan over high heat; keep warm over low heat.

2. Heat oil in large cast iron skillet over medium-high heat. Add chicken and chorizo; cook 1 minute, stirring once. Add onion, bell pepper, garlic and saffron; cook and stir 5 minutes or until vegetables are soft and chorizo is browned.

3. Stir in rice, diced tomatoes, tomato paste, salt and black pepper; cook 5 minutes, stirring occasionally. Add warm broth, ½ to 1 cup at a time, stirring after each addition until broth is almost absorbed.

4. Reduce heat to medium. Cover skillet with foil; cook 25 to 30 minutes or until rice is tender. Remove foil; gently stir in shrimp, mussels and peas. Replace foil; cook 5 to 10 minutes or until shrimp are pink and opaque and mussels open. (Discard any mussels that do not open.)

Makes 6 to 8 servings

SALMON PATTY BURGERS

1 can (about 14 ounces) red salmon, drained
1 egg white
2 tablespoons toasted wheat germ
1 tablespoon dried onion flakes
1 tablespoon capers, drained
½ teaspoon dried thyme
¼ teaspoon black pepper
1 tablespoon vegetable oil
4 whole wheat buns, split
2 tablespoons Dijon mustard
4 tomato slices
4 thin red onion slices *or* 8 dill pickle slices
4 lettuce leaves

1. Place salmon in medium bowl; mash with fork. Add egg white, wheat germ, onion flakes, capers, thyme and pepper; mix well.

2. Shape mixture into four patties; cover and refrigerate 1 hour or until firm.

3. Heat oil in large cast iron skillet over medium heat. Add patties; cook 5 minutes per side.

4. Spread cut sides of buns with mustard. Place patties on buns; top with tomato, onion, lettuce and tops of buns.

Makes 4 servings

NOTE: Red salmon is more expensive with a firm texture and deep red color. Pink salmon is less expensive with a light pink color.

SOUTHERN FRIED CATFISH WITH HUSH PUPPIES

Hush Puppy Batter (recipe follows)
4 catfish fillets (about 1½ pounds)
½ cup yellow cornmeal
3 tablespoons all-purpose flour
1½ teaspoons salt
¼ teaspoon ground red pepper
Vegetable oil for frying
Prepared remoulade or tartar sauce (optional)

1. Prepare Hush Puppy Batter; set aside.

2. Rinse catfish fillets; pat dry with paper towels. Combine cornmeal, flour, salt and red pepper in shallow bowl. Coat fish with cornmeal mixture.

3. Pour oil into large cast iron skillet to depth of 1 inch; heat to 375°F over medium heat. Cook fish in batches 4 to 5 minutes or until golden brown and fish begins to flake when tested with fork. Drain on paper towel-lined plate; keep warm. *Allow temperature of oil to return to 375°F between batches.*

4. Drop hush puppy batter by tablespoonfuls into hot oil (oil should be 375°F); cook in batches 2 minutes or until golden brown. Drain on paper towel-lined plate. Serve with catfish and sauce, if desired.

Makes 4 servings

HUSH PUPPY BATTER

1½ cups yellow cornmeal
½ cup all-purpose flour
2 teaspoons baking powder
½ teaspoon salt
1 cup milk
1 small onion, minced
1 egg, lightly beaten

Combine cornmeal, flour, baking powder and salt in medium bowl. Add milk, onion and egg; stir until well blended. Allow batter to stand 5 to 10 minutes.

Makes about 24 hush puppies

LEMON SESAME SCALLOPS

8 ounces uncooked whole wheat spaghetti

3 tablespoons sesame oil, divided

¼ cup chicken broth or clam juice

3 tablespoons lemon juice

2 tablespoons oyster sauce

1 tablespoon cornstarch

1 tablespoon soy sauce

½ teaspoon grated lemon peel

1 tablespoon vegetable oil

2 carrots, cut into thin strips

1 yellow bell pepper, cut into thin strips

4 slices peeled fresh ginger

1 clove garlic, minced

1 pound sea scallops

6 ounces fresh snow peas, trimmed, or frozen snow peas, thawed

2 green onions, thinly sliced

1 tablespoon sesame seeds, toasted*

*To toast sesame seeds, spread seeds in small skillet. Shake skillet over medium heat about 3 minutes or until seeds begin to pop and turn golden.

1. Cook spaghetti according to package directions; drain. Toss with 2 tablespoons sesame oil in medium bowl; keep warm.

2. Whisk broth, lemon juice, oyster sauce, cornstarch, soy sauce and lemon peel in small bowl until smooth and well blended; set aside.

3. Heat remaining 1 tablespoon sesame oil and vegetable oil in large cast iron skillet over medium heat. Add carrots and bell pepper; cook and stir 4 to 5 minutes or until crisp-tender. Remove to large bowl.

4. Add ginger and garlic to skillet; cook and stir 1 minute over medium-high heat. Add scallops; cook and stir 1 minute. Add snow peas and green onions; cook and stir 2 to 3 minutes or until scallops are opaque. Remove and discard ginger. Add scallop mixture to vegetable mixture in bowl, leaving any liquid in skillet.

5. Stir broth mixture into skillet; cook and stir 5 minutes or until thickened. Return scallop and vegetable mixture to skillet; cook 1 minute or until heated through. Serve scallops and vegetables over warm spaghetti. Sprinkle with sesame seeds. *Makes 4 servings*

PROSCIUTTO-WRAPPED SNAPPER

1 tablespoon plus 1 teaspoon olive oil, divided
2 cloves garlic, minced
4 skinless red snapper or halibut fillets (6 to 7 ounces each)
½ teaspoon salt
½ teaspoon black pepper
8 large fresh sage leaves
8 thin slices prosciutto (4 ounces)
¼ cup dry marsala wine

1. Preheat oven to 400°F.

2. Combine 1 tablespoon oil and garlic in small bowl; brush over snapper fillets. Sprinkle with salt and pepper. Place two sage leaves on each fillet. Wrap two prosciutto slices around fish to enclose sage leaves; tuck in ends of prosciutto.

3. Heat remaining 1 teaspoon oil in large cast iron skillet over medium-high heat. Add fish, sage side down; cook 3 to 4 minutes or until prosciutto is crisp. Carefully turn fish. Transfer skillet to oven; bake 8 to 10 minutes or until fish is opaque in center. Remove to plate; keep warm.

4. Add wine to skillet; cook over medium-high heat, scraping up browned bits from bottom of skillet. Stir constantly 2 to 3 minutes or until mixture has reduced by half. Drizzle over fish.   *Makes 4 servings*

NUTTY PAN-FRIED TROUT

2 tablespoons olive oil
½ cup seasoned dry bread crumbs
4 trout fillets (about 6 ounces each)
½ cup pine nuts

1. Heat oil in large cast iron skillet over medium heat. Place bread crumbs in shallow bowl. Coat pike fillets with bread crumbs.

2. Add fish to skillet; cook 4 minutes per side or until fish begins to flake when tested with fork. Remove to plate; keep warm.

3. Add pine nuts to drippings in skillet; cook and stir 3 minutes or until nuts are lightly toasted. Sprinkle over fish.
Makes 4 servings

Prosciutto-Wrapped Snapper

TUNA CAKES WITH CREAMY CUCUMBER SAUCE

½ cup finely chopped cucumber

½ cup plain yogurt or Greek yogurt

1½ teaspoons chopped fresh dill *or* ½ teaspoon dried dill weed

1 teaspoon lemon pepper

⅓ cup shredded carrots

¼ cup sliced green onion

¼ cup finely chopped celery

¼ cup mayonnaise

2 teaspoons spicy brown mustard

1 cup panko bread crumbs, divided

1 can (12 ounces) albacore tuna in water, drained

1½ tablespoons canola oil or olive oil, divided

Lemon wedges (optional)

1. For sauce, combine cucumber, yogurt, dill and lemon pepper in small bowl; mix well. Cover and refrigerate until ready to serve.

2. Combine carrots, green onion, celery, mayonnaise and mustard in medium bowl. Stir in ½ cup panko. Add tuna; stir until blended.

3. Place remaining ½ cup panko in shallow bowl. Shape tuna mixture into five ½-inch-thick patties. Coat patties with panko.

4. Heat 1 tablespoon oil in large cast iron skillet over medium heat. Add patties; cook 5 to 6 minutes or until golden brown, turning once and adding remaining ½ tablespoon oil to skillet when patties are turned. Serve with sauce and lemon wedges, if desired. *Makes 5 servings*

CATFISH WITH CHERRY SALSA

1 cup halved pitted fresh sweet cherries
¼ cup minced red onion
1 jalapeño pepper, seeded and minced*
1 teaspoon balsamic vinegar
¾ teaspoon salt, divided
    Pinch ground allspice
¼ cup all-purpose flour
2 tablespoons cornmeal
¼ teaspoon black pepper
¼ teaspoon paprika
⅛ teaspoon garlic salt
2 tablespoons vegetable oil
4 medium catfish fillets (about 1¼ pounds)
    Lime wedges (optional)
    Chopped fresh cilantro (optional)

*Jalapeño peppers can sting and irritate the skin, so wear rubber gloves when handling peppers and do not touch your eyes.

1. For salsa, combine cherries, red onion, jalapeño, vinegar, ½ teaspoon salt and allspice in small bowl; mix well.

2. Combine flour, cornmeal, remaining ¼ teaspoon salt, black pepper, paprika and garlic salt in shallow bowl. Coat catfish fillets with flour mixture.

3. Heat oil in large cast iron skillet over medium-high heat. Add fish; cook 4 to 5 minutes per side or until golden brown and opaque in center.

4. Serve fish with cherry salsa, lime wedges and cilantro, if desired.

Makes 4 servings

ALMOND-COATED SCALLOPS

¼ cup panko bread crumbs

2 tablespoons sliced almonds, chopped

1½ teaspoons grated lemon peel, divided

¼ teaspoon salt

⅛ teaspoon black pepper

8 jumbo sea scallops, cut in half horizontally (about 1 pound)

2½ tablespoons olive oil, divided

1 clove garlic, crushed

1. Combine panko, almonds, 1 teaspoon lemon peel, salt and pepper in shallow bowl. Brush scallops with ½ tablespoon oil; coat with panko mixture.

2. Heat remaining 2 tablespoons oil in large cast iron skillet over low heat. Add garlic; cook and stir 2 minutes. Discard garlic.

3. Add scallops to skillet in batches; cook over medium-high heat 2 to 3 minutes or until golden brown. Turn and cook 1 to 2 minutes. Sprinkle with remaining ½ teaspoon lemon peel. Serve immediately.

Makes 4 servings

CHILI GINGER SHRIMP

1 tablespoon plus 2 teaspoons soy sauce, divided

1½ tablespoons vegetable oil, divided

2 teaspoons grated fresh ginger

2 teaspoons lemon juice, divided

1 pound raw jumbo shrimp, peeled and deveined

2 tablespoons chili garlic sauce

⅛ teaspoon black pepper

2 tablespoons minced fresh cilantro

1. Combine 1 tablespoon soy sauce, ½ tablespoon oil, ginger and 1 teaspoon lemon juice in large bowl. Add shrimp; toss to coat. Cover and refrigerate 1 hour. Combine chili garlic sauce, remaining 2 teaspoons soy sauce, 1 teaspoon lemon juice and pepper in small bowl; set aside.

2. Heat remaining 1 tablespoon oil in large cast iron skillet over medium-high heat. Drain shrimp, reserving marinade. Add shrimp to skillet; cook and stir 6 minutes or until shrimp are pink and opaque.

3. Add reserved marinade and chili garlic sauce mixture to skillet; cook and stir 1 minute or until sauce boils and thickens slightly. Sprinkle with cilantro.

Makes 4 servings

Almond-Coated Scallops

VEGETABLES & SIDES

HAGGERTY

    8 slices bacon (about 8 ounces)
    3 onions, thinly sliced
1½ cups (6 ounces) shredded Irish Cheddar cheese, divided
    2 tablespoons butter, divided
    5 medium red potatoes (about 1¼ pounds), very thinly sliced
    Salt and black pepper

1. Preheat oven to 375°F.

2. Cook bacon in large cast iron skillet until crisp. Drain on paper towel-lined plate; crumble into medium bowl. Drain all but 1 tablespoon drippings from skillet.

3. Add onions to skillet; cook and stir over medium heat about 8 minutes or until translucent but not browned. Drain on paper towel-lined plate. Remove to bowl with bacon; mix well.

3. Reserve ¼ cup cheese; set aside. Melt 1 tablespoon butter in same skillet or 8- to 9-inch casserole. Arrange one quarter of potato slices to cover bottom of skillet. Season with salt and pepper. Top with one third of bacon-onion mixture; sprinkle with one third of remaining cheese. Repeat layers twice. Top with remaining one quarter of potato slices; dot with remaining 1 tablespoon butter.

4. Cover with foil and bake 50 minutes. Uncover and bake 10 minutes or until potatoes are tender. *Turn oven to broil.* Broil 2 to 3 minutes or until lightly browned. Sprinkle with reserved ¼ cup cheese. Serve warm.

Makes 6 to 8 servings

TIP: Use a mandolin to slice the potatoes very thin (about ⅛ inch). Thicker pieces may require a longer cooking time.

VEGETABLE FAJITAS WITH SPICY SALSA

3 medium tomatoes

1 small unpeeled yellow onion

1 jalapeño pepper*

6 unpeeled garlic cloves

   Juice of 1 lime

2 teaspoons salt, divided

12 flour tortillas, fajita size

1 tablespoon canola oil

4 medium bell peppers, cut into strips

1 medium red onion, peeled, cut in half vertically and thickly sliced

¼ teaspoon black pepper

1 can (16 ounces) refried beans

   Chopped fresh cilantro and sour cream (optional)

*Jalapeño peppers can sting and irritate the skin, so wear rubber gloves when handling peppers and do not touch your eyes.

1. For salsa, preheat broiler. Line baking sheet with parchment paper or foil. Place tomatoes, yellow onion, jalapeño and garlic on prepared baking sheet; broil 10 minutes. Turn vegetables and rotate pan. Broil 10 minutes or until blackened. Cool 10 minutes. Peel tomatoes, onion and garlic; peel and seed jalapeño. Place in blender or food processor with lime juice and 1 teaspoon salt; blend until desired consistency. Refrigerate until ready to serve. (Salsa can be made up to 1 week in advance.)

2. Heat large cast iron skillet over medium-high heat. Cook tortillas, one at a time, about 15 seconds per side or until blistered and browned. Keep warm.

3. Heat oil in same skillet over medium heat. Add bell peppers, red onion, remaining 1 teaspoon salt and black pepper; cook 10 minutes or until vegetables are tender, stirring occasionally.

4. Heat refried beans in small saucepan over medium heat or microwave in microwavable bowl on HIGH 1 minute, stirring occasionally. Spread 2 tablespoons beans on each tortilla; top with ⅓ cup vegetables and about 2 tablespoons salsa. Roll up tortillas; serve immediately. Garnish with cilantro and sour cream.

Makes 6 servings

CLASSIC HASH BROWNS

1 large russet potato, peeled and grated
¼ teaspoon salt
⅛ teaspoon black pepper
2 tablespoons vegetable oil

1. Squeeze liquid from potatoes in paper towels or clean kitchen towel to remove as much moisture as possible.

2. Heat medium cast iron skillet over medium heat 5 minutes. Combine potato, salt and pepper in small bowl; toss to coat.

2. Add oil to skillet; heat 30 seconds. Spread potato mixture evenly in skillet. Cook, without stirring, about 5 minutes or until bottom is browned. Turn potatoes; cook 6 to 8 minutes or until golden brown and crispy.

Makes 2 servings

CRISPY BATTERED PLANTAINS

¼ cup sugar
½ teaspoon ground cinnamon
½ cup masa harina, divided
1 egg
¼ cup cornstarch
½ cup cold water
   Vegetable oil for frying
4 large black-skinned plantains, peeled and cut into quarters

1. Combine sugar and cinnamon in medium bowl; set aside.

2. Place ¼ cup masa harina in shallow bowl. Beat egg in another shalllow bowl. Add cornstarch, remaining ¼ cup masa harina and water, blending until smooth.

3. Pour oil into large cast iron skillet to depth of 1 inch; heat to 375°F over medium-high heat. Adjust heat to maintain temperature. Coat plantains with masa harina, then with batter. Add to hot oil in batches; cook until golden brown on both sides. Drain on paper towel-lined plate.

4. Roll plantains in cinnamon-sugar. Serve warm.

Makes 8 servings

Classic Hash Browns

TANGY RED CABBAGE WITH APPLES AND BACON

  8 slices thick-cut bacon
  1 large onion, sliced
  ½ small head red cabbage (1 pound), thinly sliced
  1 tablespoon sugar
  1 Granny Smith apple, peeled and sliced
  2 tablespoons cider vinegar
  ½ teaspoon salt
  ¼ teaspoon black pepper

1. Heat large cast iron skillet over medium heat. Add bacon; cook 6 to 8 minutes or until crisp, turning occasionally. Drain on paper towel-lined plate. Coarsely chop bacon.

2. Drain all but 2 tablespoon drippings from skillet. Add onion; cook and stir over medium-high heat 2 to 3 minutes or until onion begins to soften. Add cabbage and sugar; cook and stir 4 to 5 minutes or until cabbage wilts. Stir in apple; cook 3 minutes or until crisp-tender. Stir in vinegar; cook 1 minute or until absorbed.

3. Stir in bacon, salt and pepper; cook 1 minute or until heated through. Serve warm or at room temperature.

Makes 4 servings

MASHED POTATO CAKES

  2 cups cold mashed potatoes
  ⅓ cup shredded Cheddar cheese
  3 strips bacon, crisp-cooked and crumbled
  2 egg yolks, beaten
  2 tablespoons chopped fresh parsley
  2 tablespoons snipped fresh chives
  1 tablespoon all-purpose flour
  1 teaspoon salt
  ⅛ teaspoon black pepper
  3 tablespoons vegetable oil

1. Combine mashed potatoes, cheese, bacon, egg yolks, parsley, chives, flour, salt and pepper in large bowl, mix well.

2. Heat oil in large cast iron skillet over medium heat. Scoop ¼ cupfuls of potato mixture into skillet. Cook 8 to 10 minutes per side or until golden brown.

Makes 4 servings

Tangy Red Cabbage with Apples and Bacon

CHARRED CORN SALAD

3 tablespoons fresh lime juice
½ teaspoon salt
¼ cup extra virgin olive oil
4 to 6 ears corn, husked
⅔ cup canned black beans, rinsed and drained
½ cup chopped fresh cilantro
2 teaspoons minced seeded chipotle pepper (1 canned chipotle pepper in adobo sauce *or* 1 dried chipotle pepper, reconstituted in boiling water)*

*Chipotle peppers can sting and irritate the skin, so wear rubber gloves when handling peppers and do not touch your eyes.

1. Whisk lime juice and salt in small bowl. Gradually whisk in oil. Set aside.

2. Heat large cast iron skillet over medium-high heat. Cook corn in single layer about 15 minutes or until browned and tender, turning frequently. Remove to plate to cool slightly. Slice kernels off ears and place in medium bowl.

3. Microwave beans in small microwavable bowl on HIGH 1 minute or until heated through. Add beans, cilantro and chipotle to corn; mix well. Pour lime juice mixture over corn mixture; toss to combine.

Makes 6 servings

NOTE: Chipotle peppers in adobo sauce are available canned in the ethnic section of most supermarkets. Since only a small amount is needed for this dish, spoon leftovers into a covered plastic container and refrigerate or freeze for another use.

CRISPY SKILLET POTATOES

    2 tablespoons olive oil
    4 red potatoes, cut into thin wedges
    ½ cup chopped onion
    2 tablespoons lemon pepper
    ½ teaspoon coarse salt
      Chopped fresh parsley

1. Heat oil in large cast iron skillet over medium heat. Add potatoes, onion, lemon pepper and salt; cover and cook 20 minutes, stirring occasionally. Uncover and cook 10 minutes or until potatoes are tender and browned.

2. Sprinkle with parsley just before serving.

Makes 4 servings

HONG KONG FRIED RICE CAKES

    1 package (about 6 ounces) chicken-flavored rice and vermicelli mix
    ½ cup sliced green onions
    2 eggs, beaten
    2 tablespoons chopped fresh parsley
    1 tablespoon hoisin sauce
    1 tablespoon soy sauce
    1 teaspoon minced fresh ginger
    1 clove garlic, minced
    2 to 3 tablespoons vegetable oil, divided

1. Prepare rice according to package directions, omitting butter. Cover and refrigerate 1 hour or until cold. Add green onions, eggs, parsley, hoisin sauce, soy sauce, ginger and garlic; mix well. Shape mixture into 3-inch patties.

2. Heat 1 tablespoon oil in large cast iron skillet over medium heat. Cook four patties at a time 3 to 4 minutes per side or until golden brown, adding additional oil as needed.

Makes 4 to 6 servings

Crispy Skillet Potatoes

HAVARTI AND ONION SANDWICHES

½ tablespoon olive oil
⅓ cup thinly sliced red onion
4 slices pumpernickel bread
6 ounces dill havarti cheese, cut into slices
½ cup prepared coleslaw

1. Heat oil in large cast iron skillet over medium heat. Add onion; cook and stir 5 minutes or until tender. Layer two bread slices with onion, cheese and coleslaw; top with remaining two bread slices.

2. Heat same skillet over medium heat. Add sandwiches; press down with spatula or weigh down with small plate. Cook 4 to 5 minutes per side or until cheese is melted and bread is crisp.

Makes 2 sandwiches

SMOKY BARBECUED THREE-BEAN SKILLET

1 cup chopped yellow onion
1 green or red bell pepper, diced
2 thick slices bacon, diced
1 jar (18 ounces) baked beans
1 can (15 ounces) no-salt-added red beans or kidney beans, undrained
1 can (15 ounces) no-salt-added navy beans, undrained
¼ cup ketchup
2 tablespoons packed brown sugar
2 tablespoons Dijon or yellow mustard
1 teaspoon hot pepper sauce or chipotle pepper sauce (optional)

1. Cook onion, bell pepper and bacon in large cast iron skillet over medium-high heat 6 minutes or until onion is translucent, stirring frequently.

2. Add baked beans, red beans with liquid, navy beans with liquid, ketchup, brown sugar, mustard and hot pepper sauce, if desired; bring to a simmer. Cook over medium-low heat about 10 minutes or until bell pepper is tender, stirring occasionally. *Makes 10 servings*

NOTE: The liquid from the no-salt-added beans helps to thicken this dish. You may substitute regular canned red beans and/or navy beans; however, to reduce the sodium content, you should rinse and drain the beans. As a result, the dish will not be as thick.

Havarti and Onion Sandwiches

SKILLET MAC AND CHEESE

1 pound uncooked cavatappi or rotini pasta

8 ounces thick-cut bacon, cut into ½-inch pieces

¼ cup finely chopped onion

¼ cup all-purpose flour

3½ cups whole milk

1½ cups (6 ounces) shredded fontina cheese

1 cup (4 ounces) shredded white Cheddar cheese

1 cup (4 ounces) shredded Gruyère cheese

¾ cup grated Parmesan cheese, divided

½ teaspoon salt

½ teaspoon dry mustard

¼ teaspoon ground red pepper

¼ teaspoon black pepper

¼ cup panko bread crumbs

1. Preheat oven to 400°F. Cook pasta in large saucepan according to package directions until al dente; drain.

2. Meanwhile, cook bacon in large cast iron skillet over medium heat until crisp; drain on paper towel-lined plate. Pour drippings into glass measuring cup, leaving thin coating on bottom of skillet.

3. Heat 4 tablespoons drippings in large saucepan over medium-high heat. Add onion; cook and stir about 4 minutes or until translucent. Add flour; cook and stir 5 minutes. Slowly add milk over medium-low heat, stirring constantly. Cook and stir until slightly thickened. Stir in fontina, Cheddar, Gruyère, ½ cup Parmesan, salt, mustard, red pepper and black pepper until smooth and well blended. Add cooked pasta; stir gently until coated. Stir in bacon. Spread mixture in prepared skillet.

4. Combine panko and remaining ¼ cup Parmesan in small bowl; sprinkle over pasta. Bake about 30 minutes or until top is golden brown.

Makes 6 servings

SUMMER SQUASH SKILLET

2 tablespoons butter

1 medium sweet or yellow onion, thinly sliced and separated into rings

2 medium zucchini or yellow squash (or one of each), sliced

¾ teaspoon salt

¼ teaspoon black pepper

1 large tomato, chopped

¼ cup chopped fresh basil

2 tablespoons grated Parmesan cheese

1. Heat butter in large cast iron skillet over medium-high heat. Add onion; stir to coat with butter. Cover and cook 3 minutes. Uncover; cook and stir over medium heat about 3 minutes or until onion is golden brown.

2. Add squash, salt and pepper; cover and cook 5 minutes, stirring once. Add tomato; cook uncovered about 2 minutes or until squash is tender. Stir in basil and sprinkle with cheese.   *Makes 4 servings*

BOXTY PANCAKES

2 medium russet potatoes (1 pound), peeled, divided

⅔ cup all-purpose flour

1 teaspoon baking powder

½ teaspoon salt

⅔ cup buttermilk

3 tablespoons butter

1. Cut one potato into 1-inch chunks; place in small saucepan and add cold water to cover by 2 inches. Bring to a boil over medium-high heat; cook 14 to 18 minutes or until tender. Drain potato; return to saucepan and mash. Remove to medium bowl.

2. Shred remaining potato on large holes of box grater; add to bowl with mashed potato. Stir in flour, baking powder and salt until blended. Stir in buttermilk.

3. Heat 1 tablespoon butter in large cast iron skillet over medium heat. Drop four slightly heaping tablespoonfuls of batter into skillet; flatten into 2½-inch circles. Cook about 4 minutes per side or until golden and puffed. Remove to plate; cover to keep warm. Repeat with remaining batter and butter. Serve immediately.   *Makes 4 servings (16 to 20 pancakes)*

SERVING SUGGESTION: Serve with melted butter, sour cream or maple syrup.

Summer Squash Skillet

SKILLET ROASTED ROOT VEGETABLES

1 sweet potato, peeled, halved lengthwise and cut crosswise into ½-inch slices
1 large red onion, cut into 1-inch wedges
2 parsnips, cut diagonally into 1-inch slices
2 carrots, cut diagonally into 1-inch slices
1 turnip, peeled, halved and cut crosswise into ½-inch slices
2½ tablespoons olive oil
1½ tablespoons honey
1½ tablespoons balsamic vinegar
1 teaspoon coarse salt
1 teaspoon dried thyme
¼ teaspoon ground red pepper
¼ teaspoon black pepper

1. Preheat oven to 400°F.

2. Combine all ingredients in large bowl; toss to coat. Spread vegetables in single layer in large cast iron skillet. Roast 1 hour or until vegetables are tender, stirring once halfway through cooking time.

Makes 4 servings

COUNTRY-STYLE CORN

4 slices bacon
1 tablespoon all-purpose flour
1 can (about 15 ounces) corn, drained
1 can (about 15 ounces) cream-style corn
1 red bell pepper, diced
½ cup sliced green onions
Salt and black pepper

1. Cook bacon in large cast iron skillet over medium heat until crisp; drain on paper towel-lined plate. Crumble bacon; set aside.

2. Whisk flour into drippings in skillet. Add corn, cream-style corn and bell pepper; bring to a boil. Reduce heat to low; cook 10 minutes or until thickened.

3. Stir green onions and bacon into corn mixture. Season with salt and black pepper.

Makes 6 to 8 servings

Skillet Roasted Root Vegetables

GRILLED MOZZARELLA AND ROASTED RED PEPPER SANDWICH

1 tablespoon olive oil vinaigrette or Italian salad dressing
2 slices Italian-style sandwich bread (2 ounces)
   Fresh basil leaves
⅓ cup roasted red peppers, rinsed, drained and patted dry
1 to 2 slices (1 ounce each) mozzarella or Swiss cheese
½ tablespoon olive oil

1. Brush dressing on one side of one bread slice; top with basil, roasted peppers, cheese and remaining bread slice.

2. Heat oil in large cast iron skillet over medium heat. Cook sandwich 4 to 5 minutes per side or until cheese melts and sandwich is golden brown. *Makes 1 sandwich*

STOVIES WITH BACON

3 medium russet potatoes (about 1½ pounds), peeled
6 slices bacon
2 large onions, halved vertically and sliced
4 teaspoons butter
½ teaspoon salt
⅛ teaspoon black pepper
⅓ cup water

1. Place potatoes in large saucepan; add cold water to cover by 2 inches. Bring to a boil over medium-high heat; cook 15 minutes or until partially cooked. Drain; let stand until cool enough to handle. Cut potatoes into ½-inch-thick slices.

2. Cook bacon in large cast iron skillet over medium-high heat 6 to 7 minutes or until crisp, turning occasionally. Drain on paper towel-lined plate. Chop bacon; set aside.

3. Drain all but 2 tablespoons drippings from skillet; heat over medium heat. Add onions; cook 8 to 9 minutes or until softened but not browned, stirring occasionally. Remove onions to small bowl.

4. Add butter to skillet; heat over medium heat until melted. Add potatoes; sprinkle with salt and pepper. Top with onions and water; cover and cook 5 minutes. Stir in bacon; cook, uncovered, 10 to 12 minutes or until potatoes are tender and browned, stirring occasionally. *Makes 4 servings*

Grilled Mozzarella & Roasted Red Pepper Sandwich

BALSAMIC BUTTERNUT SQUASH

    3 tablespoons olive oil
    2 tablespoons thinly sliced fresh sage (about 6 large leaves), divided
    1 medium butternut squash, peeled and cut into 1-inch pieces (4 to 5 cups)
    ½ red onion, halved and cut into ¼-inch slices
    1 teaspoon salt, divided
    2½ tablespoons balsamic vinegar
    ¼ teaspoon black pepper

1. Heat oil in large cast iron skillet over medium-high heat. Add 1 tablespoon sage; cook and stir 3 minutes. Add butternut squash, onion and ½ teaspoon salt; cook 6 minutes, stirring occasionally. (Squash should fit in crowded single layer in skillet.) Reduce heat to medium; cook 15 minutes without stirring.

2. Stir in vinegar, remaining ½ teaspoon salt and pepper; cook 10 minutes or until squash is tender, stirring occasionally. Stir in remaining 1 tablespoon sage; cook 1 minute.   *Makes 4 servings*

MOROCCAN CHICKPEAS

    1 cup chopped onion
    ¼ cup reduced-sodium vegetable broth
    2 cloves garlic, minced
    2 cans (about 15 ounces each) chickpeas, rinsed and drained
    1 can (28 ounces) diced tomatoes
    ½ cup sliced red bell pepper
    ½ cup sliced yellow bell pepper
    ½ cup sliced green bell pepper
    2 tablespoons oil-cured olives, pitted and chopped
    1 teaspoon ground cumin
    1 teaspoon ground ginger
    1 teaspoon ground turmeric
    1 bay leaf
    2 tablespoons lemon juice

1. Combine onion, broth and garlic in large cast iron skillet. Cook and stir over medium heat 3 minutes or until onion softens.

2. Stir in chickpeas, tomatoes, bell peppers, olives, cumin, ginger, turmeric and bay leaf; simmer 10 minutes or until bell peppers are tender. Remove and discard bay leaf. Stir in lemon juice; adjust seasonings.

Makes 6 servings

Balsamic Butternut Squash

SKILLET SUCCOTASH

  1 tablespoon canola oil
½ cup diced onion
½ cup diced green bell pepper
½ cup diced celery
½ teaspoon paprika
¾ cup frozen white or yellow corn
¾ cup frozen lima beans
½ cup canned diced tomatoes
  1 tablespoon minced fresh parsley
½ teaspoon salt
¼ teaspoon black pepper

1. Heat oil in large cast iron skillet over medium heat. Add onion, bell pepper and celery; cook and stir 5 minutes or until onion is translucent and bell pepper and celery are crisp-tender. Stir in paprika.

2. Add corn, lima beans and tomatoes. Reduce heat to low; cover and simmer 20 minutes or until beans are tender. Stir in parsley, salt and black pepper just before serving. *Makes 4 servings*

TIP: For additional flavor, add 1 clove minced garlic and 1 bay leaf. Remove and discard bay leaf before serving.

SWISS ROSTI POTATOES

  4 large russet potatoes (about 6 ounces each)
  4 tablespoons butter
    Salt and black pepper

1. Preheat oven to 400°F. Scrub potatoes and pierce in several places with fork. Bake 1 hour or until fork-tender. Cool completely, then refrigerate until cold.*

2. When potatoes are cold, peel with paring knife. Grate potatoes on large holes of box grater or with large grating disk of food processor.

3. Heat butter in large cast iron skillet over medium-high heat until melted and bubbly. Press grated potatoes evenly into skillet. (Do not stir or turn potatoes.) Season with salt and pepper to taste. Cook 10 to 12 minutes until golden brown.

4. Cover skillet with serving plate; invert potatoes onto plate. Serve immediately. *Makes 4 servings*

*Prepare potatoes several hours or up to 1 day in advance.

Skillet Succotash

BREADS & DESSERTS

SAUSAGE AND CHEDDAR CORN BREAD

1 tablespoon vegetable oil
½ pound bulk pork sausage
1 medium onion, diced
1 jalapeño pepper,* diced
1 package (8 ounces) corn bread and muffin mix
1 cup (4 ounces) shredded Cheddar cheese, divided
⅓ cup milk
1 egg

*Jalapeño peppers can sting and irritate the skin, so wear rubber gloves when handling peppers and do not touch your eyes.

1. Heat oil in large cast iron skillet over medium heat. Add sausage; cook until browned, stirring to break up meat. Add onion and jalapeño; cook and stir 5 minutes or until vegetables are softened. Remove to medium bowl.

2. Preheat oven to 350°F. Combine corn bread mix, ½ cup cheese, milk and egg in separate medium bowl. Pour batter into skillet. Spread sausage mixture over batter; sprinkle with remaining ½ cup cheese.

3. Bake 20 to 25 minutes or until edges are lightly browned. Cut into wedges. Refrigerate leftovers.

Makes 10 servings

CHAPATIS

2 cups whole wheat flour (or a combination of whole wheat and all-purpose flour)
1 tablespoon vegetable oil
1 teaspoon salt
¾ to 1 cup warm water

1. Combine flour, oil and salt in food processor. With motor running, drizzle ¾ cup water through feed tube until dough forms a ball that cleans side of bowl. Let dough stand 1 to 2 minutes.

2. Turn on processor and slowly add additional water until dough is soft but not sticky. If dough is hard or dry, cut into quarters and sprinkle water over quarters. Process until dough forms a soft ball, gradually adding additional water if dough will absorb it. Let dough stand in work bowl 5 minutes.

3. Turn dough onto lightly greased surface; shape into a ball. Cover and let stand at room temperature about 1 hour.

4. Divide dough into 16 equal pieces. Roll out each piece into 6- to 8-inch thin circle on lightly floured surface.

5. Heat large cast iron skillet over medium heat until hot enough to sizzle a drop of water. Cook each chapati about 1 minute per side or until golden. (Press down dough with wide spatula to cook evenly.) Serve hot.

Makes 16 chapatis

TIP

Chapati, also known as roti, is an unleavened flatbread common in northern India and Pakistan. Chaptis are often served with meals; pieces are torn off and used to scoop up small amounts of meat or vegetable dishes.

CINNAMON PECAN ROLLS

¼ cup (½ stick) butter, melted, divided
1 loaf (1 pound) frozen bread dough, thawed
½ cup packed dark brown sugar
2 teaspoons ground cinnamon
½ cup chopped pecans

1. Brush large cast iron skillet with ½ tablespoon melted butter. Roll out dough into 18×8-inch rectangle on lightly floured surface.

2. Combine brown sugar, 3 tablespoons butter and cinnamon in medium bowl; mix well. Brush mixture evenly over dough; sprinkle with pecans. Starting with long side, roll up tightly jelly-roll style. Pinch seam to seal.

3. Cut crosswise into 1-inch slices; arrange slices cut side down in prepared skillet. Cover loosely with plastic wrap. Let rise in warm place about 30 minutes or until doubled in bulk.

4. Preheat oven to 350°F. Brush tops of rolls with remaining ½ tablespoon butter. Bake 20 to 25 minutes or until golden brown. Serve warm. *Makes 18 rolls*

VARIATIONS: If desired, sprinkle ½ cup raisins over the dough instead of or in addition to the pecans before rolling it up. For an extra rich treat, sprinkle with ½ cup semisweet chocolate chips.

TIP: For a quick and easy icing, whisk ½ cup powdered sugar and 1 tablespoon milk in a small bowl until smooth. Drizzle over warm rolls.

CONFETTI CORN BREAD

3½ tablespoons vegetable oil, divided
1½ cups all-purpose flour
¾ cup yellow cornmeal
2 tablespoons sugar
1 tablespoon baking powder
1 teaspoon baking soda
¾ teaspoon salt
½ teaspoon black pepper
1⅓ cups buttermilk
½ cup finely chopped red bell pepper
1 tablespoon dried chives or dried onion flakes
1 cup corn
¾ cup (3 ounces) shredded Cheddar cheese

1. Preheat oven to 425°F. Brush 10-inch deep cast iron skillet with ½ tablespoon oil. Place in oven to heat.

2. Combine flour, cornmeal, sugar, baking powder, baking soda, salt and black pepper in large bowl; mix well. Combine buttermilk, bell pepper, remaining 3 tablespoons oil and chives in 2-cup glass measure.

3. Make well in center of flour mixture; add buttermilk mixture and stir just until dry ingredients are moistened. *Do not overmix.* Fold in corn and cheese. Spoon batter into hot skillet.

4. Bake 20 to 25 minutes or until toothpick inserted into center comes out clean. Cut into wedges; serve immediately.

Makes 12 servings

BASIL BISCUITS

   2 cups all-purpose flour

   4 tablespoons grated Parmesan cheese, divided

   1 tablespoon baking powder

   ½ teaspoon baking soda

   ¼ teaspoon salt

   4 tablespoons cream cheese

2½ tablespoons butter, divided

   6 ounces plain yogurt

   ⅓ cup slivered fresh basil leaves

1. Preheat oven to 375°F.

2. Combine flour, 2 tablespoons Parmesan, baking powder, baking soda and salt in large bowl. Cut in cream cheese and 1 tablespoon butter with pastry blender or two knives until mixture resembles coarse crumbs. Stir in yogurt and basil, mixing just until dough clings together. Turn dough out onto lightly floured surface and gently pat into a ball. Knead just until dough holds together. Pat and roll dough into 7-inch log. Cut into 7 (1-inch-thick) slices.

3. Melt remaining 1½ tablespoons butter. Brush 10-inch cast iron skillet with ½ tablespoon butter. Arrange biscuits in single layer in skillet; brush with 1 tablespoon melted butter. Sprinkle with remaining 2 tablespoons Parmesan.

4. Bake 20 to 30 minutes or until golden and firm. *Makes 7 biscuits*

WARM MIXED BERRY PIE

2 packages (12 ounces each) frozen mixed berries, thawed and drained
⅓ cup sugar
3 tablespoons cornstarch
2 teaspoons grated orange peel
¼ teaspoon ground ginger
1 refrigerated pie crust (half of 14-ounce package)

1. Preheat oven to 350°F.

2. Combine berries, sugar, cornstarch, orange peel and ginger in large bowl; toss to coat. Spoon into large cast iron skillet. Place crust over filling; crimp edge as desired.

3. Bake 1 hour or until crust is golden brown. Let stand 1 hour before serving.   *Makes 8 servings*

BANANAS FLAMBÉ

2 tablespoons butter
½ teaspoon ground cinnamon
2 small firm ripe bananas, peeled and cut in half crosswise
2 tablespoons frozen unsweetened apple juice concentrate
2 tablespoons brandy or cognac

1. Heat butter in large cast iron skillet over medium heat. Stir in cinnamon. Add bananas; cook about 1 minute per side or until heated through. Add apple juice concentrate; cook 1 minute, stirring occasionally. Drizzle with brandy; remove from heat. Carefully ignite with lighted match; shake skillet until flames are extinguished.

2. Transfer bananas to individual dessert dishes, reserving liquid in skillet. Cook liquid over medium-high heat about 1 minute or until thickened and bubbly. Pour over bananas; serve immediately.

Makes 2 servings

Warm Mixed Berry Pie

CHOCOLATE-STUFFED DOUGHNUTS

½ cup semisweet chocolate chips
2 tablespoons whipping cream
1 package (7½ ounces) refrigerated buttermilk biscuits (10 count)
½ cup granulated or powdered sugar
¾ cup vegetable oil

1. Combine chocolate chips and cream in small microwavable bowl. Microwave on HIGH 20 seconds; stir until smooth. Cover and refrigerate 1 hour or until firm.

2. Separate dough into individual biscuits. Using melon baller or small teaspoon, scoop out 1 rounded teaspoon chocolate mixture; place in center of each biscuit. Press dough around chocolate and pinch to form a ball. Roll pinched end on work surface to seal dough and flatten ball slightly.

3. Place sugar in shallow bowl. Heat oil in medium cast iron skillet until hot but not smoking. Cook doughnuts in small batches about 30 seconds per side or until golden brown. Drain on paper towel-lined plate.

4. Roll warm doughnuts in sugar to coat. Serve warm or at room temperature. (Doughnuts are best within a few hours of cooking.) *Makes 10 doughnuts*

TIP: For a quicker chocolate filling, use chocolate chips instead of the chocolate-cream mixture. Place 6 to 8 chips in the center of each biscuit; proceed with shaping and cooking doughnuts as directed.

INDIVIDUAL FRIED APPLE CRANBERRY PIES

3 tablespoons butter

3 Gala apples (about 12 ounces), peeled and diced

3 tablespoons dried cranberries

3 tablespoons packed brown sugar

1½ tablespoons lemon juice

¾ teaspoon ground cinnamon

¼ teaspoon ground nutmeg

⅛ teaspoon salt

1 package (about 14 ounces) refrigerated pie crusts

Vegetable oil for frying

Powdered sugar

1. Heat butter in large cast iron skillet over medium heat. Add apples; cook 8 minutes, stirring frequently. Add cranberries, brown sugar, lemon juice, cinnamon, nutmeg and salt; cook and stir 4 minutes or until apples are tender. Remove to medium bowl; cool 15 minutes. Wipe out skillet.

2. Let crusts stand at room temperature 15 minutes. Heat 2 cups oil to 350°F in same skillet over medium heat.

3. Roll out each crust into 12½-inch circle on floured surface; cut out seven 4-inch circles from each crust. Place generous tablespoon apple mixture on half of one dough circle, leaving ¼-inch border. Dip finger in water and moisten edge of dough circle. Fold dough over filling, pressing lightly. Dip fork in flour and crimp edge of dough to seal completely. Repeat with remaining dough and filling.

4. Working in batches, cook pies 1 minute. Turn and cook 1 minute or until lightly browned. Remove to paper-towel lined baking sheet. Allow oil temperature to return to 350°F between batches.

5. Sprinkle with powdered sugar; serve warm or at room temperature.   *Makes 14 pies*

NOTE: Granny Smith apples can be substituted for Gala apples. Increase brown sugar to 4 tablespoons and replace lemon juice with water.

CHOCOLATE CHIP SKILLET COOKIE

1¾ cups all-purpose flour
1 teaspoon baking soda
1 teaspoon salt
¾ cup (1½ sticks) butter, softened
¾ cup packed brown sugar
½ cup granulated sugar
2 eggs
1 teaspoon vanilla
1 package (12 ounces) semisweet chocolate chips
Sea salt (optional)
Ice cream (optional)

1. Preheat oven to 350°F.

2. Combine flour, baking soda and 1 teaspoon salt in medium bowl. Beat butter, brown sugar and granulated sugar in large bowl with electric mixer at medium speed until creamy. Beat in eggs and vanilla until well blended. Gradually beat in flour mixture at low speed just until blended. Stir in chocolate chips. Press dough evenly into well-seasoned* 10-inch cast iron skillet. Sprinkle lightly with sea salt, if desired.

3. Bake about 35 minutes or until top and edges are golden brown but cookie is still soft in center. Cool on wire rack 10 minutes before cutting into wedges. Serve warm with ice cream, if desired.

Makes 8 servings

*If skillet is not well seasoned, brush with 1 tablespoon melted butter.

TIP

Even better than a warm wedge of skillet cookie is a personal skillet cookie! You can find small (4- to 6-inch) cast iron skillets at kitchenware and home goods stores—they are inexpensive and perfect for making individual servings. You can use them for other desserts such as mini pies and crisps; they can also be used for single servings of casseroles and pot pies.

GINGER PLUM TART

    1 refrigerated pie crust (half of 14-ounce package)
1¾ pounds plums, cut into ½-inch slices
    ½ cup plus 1 teaspoon sugar, divided
1½ tablespoons all-purpose flour
1½ teaspoons ground ginger
    ¼ teaspoon ground cinnamon
    ⅛ teaspoon salt
    1 egg
    2 teaspoons water

1. Preheat oven to 400°F. Let crust stand at room temperature 10 minutes. Combine plums, ½ cup sugar, flour, ginger, cinnamon and salt in large bowl; toss to coat.

2. Roll out crust into 14-inch circle on lightly floured surface. Transfer to 10-inch cast iron skillet. Mound plum mixture in center of crust, leaving 2-inch border around fruit. Fold crust up over filling, pleating as necessary and gently pressing crust into fruit.

3. Beat egg and water in small bowl; brush over crust. Sprinkle with remaining 1 teaspoon sugar.

4. Bake about 45 minutes or until crust is golden brown. *Makes 6 to 8 servings*

CHERRY CLAFOUTI

    1 tablespoon butter, softened
    1 cup whole milk
    4 eggs
    ½ cup all-purpose flour
    ½ cup packed brown sugar
    1 teaspoon vanilla
    ¼ teaspoon salt
    1 package (1 pound) frozen dark sweet cherries, thawed, drained and patted dry

1. Preheat oven to 350°F. Grease 10-inch cast iron skillet with butter.

2. Combine milk, eggs, flour, brown sugar, vanilla and salt in blender; blend until smooth. Pour batter into prepared skillet; sprinkle cherries over batter.

3. Bake about 35 minutes or until set, puffed and golden brown and toothpick inserted into center comes out clean. *Makes 8 servings*

Ginger Plum Tart

HONEY SOPAIPILLAS

¼ cup plus 2 teaspoons sugar, divided
½ teaspoon ground cinnamon
 2 cups all-purpose flour
½ teaspoon salt
 2 teaspoons baking powder
 2 tablespoons shortening
¾ cup warm water
   Vegetable oil for frying
   Honey

1. Combine ¼ cup sugar and cinnamon in small bowl; set aside. Combine remaining 2 teaspoons sugar, flour, salt and baking powder in large bowl. Cut in shortening with pastry blender or two knives until mixture resembles fine crumbs. Gradually add water; stir with fork until mixture forms dough. Turn out onto lightly floured surface; knead 2 minutes or until smooth. Shape into a ball; cover with bowl and let rest 30 minutes.

2. Divide dough into four equal pieces; shape each into a ball. Flatten each ball into 8-inch circle about ⅛ inch thick. Cut each round into four wedges.

3. Pour oil into large cast iron skillet to depth of 1½ inches; heat to 360°F over medium-high heat. Adjust heat to maintain temperature. Cook two pieces of dough at a time 2 minutes or until puffed and golden brown, turning once. Remove with slotted spoon; drain on paper towel-lined plate. Sprinkle with cinnamon-sugar mixture. Serve hot with honey. *Makes 16 sopaipillas*

NOTE: Sopaipillas are a New Mexican specialty, originating in Albuquerque more than 200 years ago. These deep-fried pockets of dough may be served with meals instead of bread or used as a pocket for stuffing with taco fillings. (Omit the cinnamon-sugar and honey.) The most popular way to enjoy sopaipillas is for dessert, served with honey.

APPLE CRANBERRY CRUMBLE

4 large apples (about 1⅓ pounds), peeled and cut into ¼-inch slices
2 cups fresh or frozen cranberries
⅓ cup granulated sugar
6 tablespoons all-purpose flour, divided
1 teaspoon apple pie spice, divided
¼ teaspoon salt, divided
½ cup chopped walnuts
¼ cup old-fashioned oats
2 tablespoons packed brown sugar
¼ cup (½ stick) butter, cut into small pieces

1. Preheat oven to 375°F.

2. Combine apples, cranberries, granulated sugar, 2 tablespoons flour, ½ teaspoon apple pie spice and ⅛ teaspoon salt in large bowl; toss to coat. Transfer to medium cast iron skillet.

3. For topping, combine remaining ¼ cup flour, walnuts, oats, brown sugar, remaining ½ teaspoon apple pie spice and ⅛ teaspoon salt in medium bowl; mix well. Cut in butter with pastry blender or two knives until mixture resembles coarse crumbs. Spread over fruit in skillet.

4. Bake 50 to 60 minutes or until filling is bubbly and topping is lightly browned.   *Makes 4 servings*

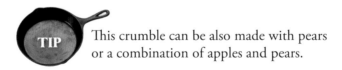

TIP This crumble can be also made with pears or a combination of apples and pears.

METRIC CONVERSION CHART

VOLUME MEASUREMENTS (dry)

$\frac{1}{8}$ teaspoon = 0.5 mL
$\frac{1}{4}$ teaspoon = 1 mL
$\frac{1}{2}$ teaspoon = 2 mL
$\frac{3}{4}$ teaspoon = 4 mL
1 teaspoon = 5 mL
1 tablespoon = 15 mL
2 tablespoons = 30 mL
$\frac{1}{4}$ cup = 60 mL
$\frac{1}{3}$ cup = 75 mL
$\frac{1}{2}$ cup = 125 mL
$\frac{2}{3}$ cup = 150 mL
$\frac{3}{4}$ cup = 175 mL
1 cup = 250 mL
2 cups = 1 pint = 500 mL
3 cups = 750 mL
4 cups = 1 quart = 1 L

VOLUME MEASUREMENTS (fluid)

1 fluid ounce (2 tablespoons) = 30 mL
4 fluid ounces ($\frac{1}{2}$ cup) = 125 mL
8 fluid ounces (1 cup) = 250 mL
12 fluid ounces (1$\frac{1}{2}$ cups) = 375 mL
16 fluid ounces (2 cups) = 500 mL

WEIGHTS (mass)

$\frac{1}{2}$ ounce = 15 g
1 ounce = 30 g
3 ounces = 90 g
4 ounces = 120 g
8 ounces = 225 g
10 ounces = 285 g
12 ounces = 360 g
16 ounces = 1 pound = 450 g

DIMENSIONS

$\frac{1}{16}$ inch = 2 mm
$\frac{1}{8}$ inch = 3 mm
$\frac{1}{4}$ inch = 6 mm
$\frac{1}{2}$ inch = 1.5 cm
$\frac{3}{4}$ inch = 2 cm
1 inch = 2.5 cm

OVEN TEMPERATURES

250°F = 120°C
275°F = 140°C
300°F = 150°C
325°F = 160°C
350°F = 180°C
375°F = 190°C
400°F = 200°C
425°F = 220°C
450°F = 230°C

BAKING PAN SIZES

Utensil	Size in Inches/Quarts	Metric Volume	Size in Centimeters
Baking or Cake Pan (square or rectangular)	8×8×2	2 L	20×20×5
	9×9×2	2.5 L	23×23×5
	12×8×2	3 L	30×20×5
	13×9×2	3.5 L	33×23×5
Loaf Pan	8×4×3	1.5 L	20×10×7
	9×5×3	2 L	23×13×7
Round Layer Cake Pan	8×1½	1.2 L	20×4
	9×1½	1.5 L	23×4
Pie Plate	8×1¼	750 mL	20×3
	9×1¼	1 L	23×3
Baking Dish or Casserole	1 quart	1 L	—
	1½ quart	1.5 L	—
	2 quart	2 L	—